Everything
Will Be
Okay

T0016838

Jean Fischer

Everything Will Be Okay

Courage-Building Devotions & Prayers for Kids

BARBOUR **kidz**

A Division of Barbour Publishing

Published by Barbour Publishing, Inc., 1810 Barbour Drive, Uhrichsville, Ohio 44683, www.barbourbooks.com

Our mission is to inspire the world with the life-changing message of the Bible.

 Member of the Evangelical Christian Publishers Association

Printed in China.

001722 0923 HA

INTRODUCTION

New goals, new places, hellos, goodbyes, family stuff, friend stuff, school stuff, things in the news stuff. . . Sometimes, the world is so overstuffed, it makes you wonder, *Will everything be okay?* God says, "Yes!" Our God, the God of everything, loves you and watches over you. When something worries you, you can talk with Him and ask for help. If trouble stresses you out, you can trust God to give you courage and strength to handle it. The Bible says God will give you a sense of everything coming together for good that will settle you down in a wonderful way (see Philippians 4:6–7 MSG). Everyone feels worried and afraid sometimes. But with God on your side, everything will be okay.

" 'For I know the plans I have for you,' says the Lord, 'plans for well-being and not for trouble, to give you a future and a hope.' "
JEREMIAH 29:11

WHEN I'M AFRAID

"Do not be afraid, just believe."

MARK 5:36

If you feel afraid sometimes, you aren't alone. Everyone is afraid of something. We all get that fluttery sick feeling in our stomachs that makes us want to run. When you feel afraid, it helps to remember that God is with you. When He made you, God planned each day of your life. He knows everything about you right down to the number of hairs on your head! The Bible says God is love (1 John 4:8), and when He planned your life, He did it in the most loving way. God doesn't want you to be afraid that you will fall flat on your face when you try something new. He doesn't want you to run away when you feel afraid or give up when you fail. He promises to help you be strong and brave. God loves you. He is with you always, and He will guide you through every day.

Dear God, I believe You love me and are always with me. I will trust You to guide and help me, especially when I feel afraid. Amen.

WHEN I'M SAD

Then Jesus cried.

JOHN 11:35

When Jesus lived on earth, He had human feelings like yours. He sometimes felt happy, disappointed, tired, hungry, calm, annoyed, and lonely—just like you do. Jesus felt sad sometimes too. The Bible says that when His friend Lazarus died, Jesus cried. Jesus lives in heaven now, but He remembers what it feels like to be human. He knows all your emotions, and He sees when you cry. The Bible says God has a bottle in which He keeps all your tears and a book in which He writes down how many you shed (Psalm 56:8). Whether something you hoped for didn't happen, your team lost a close and important game, someone said something mean to you, things went badly at school, or someone you loved died, remember—Jesus knows how you feel. He understands. Go someplace quiet and tell Him about it. He's ready to listen.

Dear Jesus, when I feel sad, talking with You helps me to feel better. Thank You for listening and for comforting me. Amen.

NOBODY UNDERSTANDS ME!

"Then you will call upon Me and come and
pray to Me, and I will listen to you."

JEREMIAH 29:12

Do you feel like nobody understands you? Most kids do. There will be times when you can't put into words exactly how you feel. When you talk with God about it, you don't have to use special words. You can simply say, "Dear God, nobody understands." You can pour out all your troubles to Him or you can say nothing at all and just sit quietly in His presence. If you're in a bad mood, that's okay; God understands. He wants to hear from you anyway. He's never too far away or too busy to listen. Even when you don't know the reason why you feel unsettled, God knows. He understands everything about you, and He hears every prayer. Get in the habit of talking with Him. It isn't necessary to say your words out loud. Even when you pray silently, God hears.

Dear God, nobody understands why I'm upset today, but
You know what's bothering me. Let's talk about it. Amen.

DOES GOD REALLY HEAR ME?

*As for me, I will call on God. . . . I will cry out and complain in
the evening and morning and noon, and He will hear my voice.*

PSALM 55:16–17

You can be sure God hears your prayers, because the Bible says so
(Jeremiah 29:12–13). Everything in the Bible is true. As you read it
from beginning to end, you'll find God hearing and talking with His
people. God promises to hear you too. You can trust in His promise
because God is perfect. Every word He speaks and every promise
He makes is true. God has the amazing power to be everywhere all
the time (Jeremiah 23:23–24). He sees you wherever you are, and
He hears what you say. God knows your thoughts too. He hears
them just as if you were saying them out loud. What makes your
relationship with God different from any other is that although you
can't see or hear Him, God can see and hear you!

Dear God, help me to trust that You'll hear every prayer. Amen.

WHAT IS FAITH?

Men cannot say they do not know about God.
From the beginning of the world, men could see what
God is like through the things He has made.

ROMANS 1:20

The next time someone is speaking to you, close your eyes and listen. You can't see the person who's speaking, but you know the speaker is there. Faith is believing in something you can't see. You can't see the air you breathe, but it's there keeping you alive. You can't see God either, but there is evidence of Him all around you. God created everything. When you look at the sky and see the stars, beautiful sunrises and sunsets; when you plant a seed and watch it grow to produce a vegetable or flower—that's evidence of God being real and at work. Can you think of other things that help you believe God exists?

Dear God, I can't see You, but I feel You all around me. When I pray, I know You are there because I feel like I'm talking to my best friend. By faith I know You exist. Amen.

WHO'S IN CONTROL?

I have put my trust in God. I will not be afraid.

PSALM 56:4

Think about this: You only have control over some of the things you worry about. For example, if you're worried because you and a friend aren't getting along, you have some control over the situation because you can talk with your friend about the problem or maybe change your behavior. If you're worried about your grades, you can work harder and get help for whatever you don't understand. Bigger worries, though, often belong to God. You can't control things like storms, floods, and fires. You can't change how someone else feels or behaves. You can't predict what will happen tomorrow, next week, or next year. God doesn't want you stressed out over things you can't control, so practice trusting Him with those big things and also with the little things. When you trust God to help you with every worry, you will learn to worry less and trust Him more.

Dear God, help me to know what I can control and what I can't. Help me to trust You with all my worries. Amen.

TRUST GOD

Do not worry. Learn to pray about everything.
Give thanks to God as you ask Him for what you need.

Worry is like a grumpy-all-the-time person who spoils the fun. Worry stops you from trying, having adventures, taking safe chances, and learning something new. It fills your stomach with butterflies and makes you feel sick. It gives you a headache. Worry tells you to run away or hide in your room. If you give in to worry, then you'll miss out on all the good stuff. God has so many wonderful new things waiting for you if you trust Him to keep you safe and sound. Maybe there's something new you would like to try but worry is getting in your way. Ask God to help you be brave enough to take the first step. Tell worry to move along. Then trust God to guide you.

Dear God, I don't want to be worried or afraid to try something new. Please give me courage. Let's give it a try together. Amen.

TURN IT AROUND

Keep your minds thinking about whatever is true, whatever is respected, whatever is right, whatever is pure, whatever can be loved, and whatever is well thought of. If there is anything good and worth giving thanks for, think about these things.

PHILIPPIANS 4:8

You can start doing things right now to chase away your worries. When something worrisome pops into your brain, squash that thought! Turn it around by thinking about something good. You have so much to be grateful for. Think about those things, and while you are thinking, thank God for them. Do your best to flip any negative thoughts to positive. If the worries stick with you, do something to get your mind off them like volunteering to help someone in need. Worries move along when you turn your thoughts from yourself to others. Every day, give your worries to God and have hope that He is working on your problems. Trust in Him that everything will be okay.

Dear God, please guide my thoughts away from worry and toward You and others. Amen.

PERFECTLY WONDERFUL YOU

I praise you because of the wonderful way you created me.

PSALM 139:14 CEV

Getting rid of worries has a lot to do with how you feel about yourself. How often do you look in the mirror and say, "I'm so awesome!" God made you to be awesome. He created you exactly the way He wanted you to be. What you see in the mirror is what's on the outside—your hair, facial features, and skin. But what God put inside your heart makes you even more awesome. He made you to be strong, confident, caring, brave, adventurous, and resourceful. He made you to be calm, capable, helpful, hardworking, and so much more. When you flip thoughts that say, "I'm not okay" to "I like who I am!" then you will be more able to face your worries head-on with confidence and strength.

Dear God, I can be hard on myself sometimes. Help me to see myself the way You see me. I am perfect in Your sight. You made me awesome, just as I am. Amen.

STAND UP TO TROUBLE

"The Lord is my Helper. I am not afraid
of anything man can do to me."
HEBREWS 13:6

The Bible tells the story of a young boy, David, who was courageous, confident, and brave. When all the soldiers in the Israelites' army were afraid of a huge, hulking enemy soldier named Goliath, David wasn't frightened. He marched right up to the big guy and knocked him down by throwing one single stone. When trouble stands in your way, remember David. Tell yourself, "I'm courageous. I'll stand up to trouble and knock it down." And remember too that God is on your side. You will never fight trouble alone because God is always with you. When trouble comes your way, trust God to give you courage and strength. The two of you will fight it together.

Dear God, I often think of trouble as being bigger and stronger than I am. Make me brave and give me strength to stand up to trouble. You are my all-the-time helper. I am never alone. Amen.

YES, I CAN!

*When we have learned not to give up, it shows we have stood
the test. When we have stood the test, it gives us hope.*

ROMANS 5:4

Can you think of a time when you gave up because something was too hard? If you give up, you're telling yourself, "I can't." Telling yourself "I can't" too often leads to losing confidence in yourself. And if you lose confidence in yourself, you might decide to walk away from the hard stuff and not even try. One way to feel really good about yourself is to keep trying until you succeed. Finally accomplishing something after trying again and again feels amazing. If something seems impossible, God is ready to help. Ask Him to show you what to do. If you stay hopeful, God will guide you toward turning an "I can't" into "Yes, I can!"

---

*Dear God, I feel frustrated. I keep trying, but it's
not working. Show me what to do. Give me strength
to keep at it and help me to succeed. Amen.*

TAKE THAT FIRST STEP

"Call to Me, and I will answer you. And I will show you great and wonderful things which you do not know."

JEREMIAH 33:3

God has many exciting adventures waiting for you, but you have to be willing to take the first step. There was a time when no one knew what was on the moon. People were curious. They wanted to know what was up there. Because scientists kept trying and never gave up, the day came when astronauts landed on the moon. They weren't afraid of having an adventure! They trusted that it would be okay. When Neil Armstrong first stepped onto the moon, he said, "That's one small step for a man, one giant leap for mankind." What adventures do you imagine having? Would you be brave enough to take the first step into the unknown? God will be your guide. Let Him lead you to discover great and wonderful things.

Dear God, there are adventures I'd like to have, but I'm afraid to try. Help me to take the first step. I know You will be there guiding me and holding my hand. Amen.

RELATIONSHIPS

" 'You must love the Lord your God with all your heart and with all your soul and with all your mind and with all your strength.' This is the first Law. The second Law is this: 'You must love your neighbor as yourself. No other Law is greater than these.' "

MARK 12:30–31

Maybe you have a friendship that's not going well or you're having trouble with a teacher or coach. You might even be worried about a relationship that's out of your control—for example, your parents getting along or a problem between a parent and a relative. Jesus said there are two important laws about relationships: first, love God with your whole heart, and second, do your best to love others. Loving God is the easier part. Loving others can be hard, especially when the relationship isn't going well. Ask God to help you become more loving. Ask for His help when you need to stop worrying about relationships you can't control.

Dear God, teach me to love You more and to love others, especially when we aren't getting along. Amen.

MY VERY BEST FRIEND

*A man who has friends must be a friend, but there
is a friend who stays nearer than a brother.*

PROVERBS 18:24

Everyone has days when their world seems upside down and all
messed up. On days like that, you need a friend. Who is your best
friend? Maybe it's someone from your church or school, a friend
in your neighborhood, or a family member. As awesome as your
best friend is, there is someone even more awesome. His name is
Jesus! On good days, bad days, and every day in between, Jesus is
your very best friend. Wherever you are, He's right there with you.
Jesus always has time for you. He cares for you and is ready to help
whenever you need it. Jesus wants you to have many good friends,
and if you put Him first, He will lead you to them. What kind of
person do you think would be a good friend?

---

*Dear Jesus, thank You for being my very best friend.
Help me to find friends who know and love You. Amen.*

ALL KINDS OF FRIENDS

God does not see you as a Jew or as a Greek. He does not see
you as a servant or as a person free to work. He does not see
you as a man or as a woman. You are all one in Christ.
GALATIANS 3:28

If you ask Jesus to help you find new friends, you might be surprised
where He leads you. It's good to have friends whom you have a lot
in common with, but the friends you will learn the most from are
those who are different. You eat meat; your friend is a vegetarian.
You wear your hair in a shag; your friend's hairstyle is tight curls.
Your friend has five siblings; you have none. You were born in the
town where you live; your friend was born in another country. There
are many ways friends are different and yet one important way they
are alike—God made them all! When you look for new friends, look
for those who share your same values and behave to please God.

Dear God, thank You for making us different. Amen.

LEFT OUT

He heals those who have a broken heart. He heals their sorrows.

PSALM 147:3

Wherever you are—in class, at church doing group activities, or in the lunchroom eating with your friends—look around for kids who are left out. Keep your eyes open, and you're sure to find someone who looks a little uncomfortable. Maybe it's a new kid in school or a kid who's always quiet. It might be someone who doesn't make friends easily or someone who looks sad. Jesus noticed people who were left out, and He welcomed them in. You can do the same. Be a friend to those who don't have many friends. Introduce them to your friends and invite them to join in your fun. Help them to see that there's nothing to be afraid of and that everything's going to be okay. If you're someone who feels left out, tell a parent or another trusted adult. They might have ideas to help you.

Dear God, open my eyes to those who are left out.
Help me to be welcoming, like Jesus. Amen.

COMPARISONS

We are His work. He has made us to belong to
Christ Jesus so we can work for Him.

Ephesians 2:10

Is there someone you admire, and you think to yourself, *I wish I were more like him [or her]*? Jesus is someone to admire. If you want to be more like Him, you're headed in the right direction. It's great to see positive things in others and want those qualities to be part of your personality. But be careful you don't compare yourself with others and wish you looked different, were more popular, smarter, taller, talented. . .Remember, God made you unique and special. You are one of a kind, and He put everything good inside your heart that makes you perfectly you. Can you name five good things about yourself? Get in the habit of thinking about all your wonderful qualities, and do your best to put away the comparisons.

Dear God, You made me unique and special. You put inside my
heart everything I need to become more like Jesus. Amen.

TOO TALL, TOO SMALL

But the Lord said. . ."Do not look at the way he looks on the outside or how tall he is. . . . For the Lord does not look at the things man looks at. A man looks at the outside of a person, but the Lord looks at the heart."

1 SAMUEL 16:7

There are people who look at others and see too tall, too short, too big, too small—they allow all those "too's" to get in the way of seeing a person's heart. God told a man named Samuel, "Don't look at the way people look on the outside. Be more like Me. Look at what's inside the heart." God wasn't speaking of the organ in your chest that pumps your blood. He meant the soul, the heart of who you are. That's the part that holds all your feelings, hopes, and wants. Instead of focusing on how people look on the outside, look deeper. Find out what's in their hearts.

Dear God, I don't want to judge others by their outward appearance. Help me to look at their hearts. Amen.

TOO YOUNG

But the Lord said to me, "Do not say, 'I am only a boy.' You must go everywhere I send you. And you must say whatever I tell you."

JEREMIAH 1:7

Have you ever seen a problem and said, "I wish I could do something about that, but I'm too young?" Jeremiah, in the Bible, felt that way. He was just a kid when God gave him a big responsibility. "But I'm only a boy!" Jeremiah complained. "Don't say that," God answered. "Go where I send you. Say what I tell you." If you think you're too young to be useful or to make a difference, remember what God told Jeremiah. Trust God to lead you. Think of one thing you can do to make things better at home or at school. What can you do to help your community become even better? You're never too young to make a difference. Kids like you have great ideas. Put your ideas into action, and ask God to guide you.

Dear God, how can I make a difference?
Show me what to do. Amen.

BE DIFFERENT

*Do not act like the sinful people of the world. Let God
change your life. First of all, let Him give you a new mind.
Then you will know what God wants you to do. And the
things you do will be good and pleasing and perfect.*

ROMANS 12:2

Everyone wants to feel comfortable in a group. They want to fit
in and be accepted. With friends who share your ideas of what's
right and wrong, fitting in can be easy. But if you hang around with
friends whose values aren't like yours, you might feel out of place.
You have a choice. You can change your values to fit theirs, or you
can be brave enough to be different. If your friends pull you away
from God, turn around. Find friends who know God and will lead
you nearer to Him. God put a sense of what's right and wrong inside
your heart. Be brave enough to be different instead of following
the crowd.

---

*Dear God, I don't mind being different if it
leads me nearer to You. Amen.*

DEAR GOD, I MESSED UP!

*If we tell [God] our sins, He is faithful and we can depend on Him
to forgive us of our sins. He will make our lives clean from all sin.*

1 JOHN 1:9

You messed up. You said or did something without thinking, and
now you're sorry. Maybe you're wondering if God is angry with you.
After all, He sees and knows everything you do. The good news is
that God loves you and will always forgive you. You don't need to be
afraid or to hide from God after you mess up. When you pray, tell
God what you did. Then say you're sorry. Right that very minute,
God will forgive you! He doesn't keep track of how many times you
mess up. God knows you're human, and humans make mistakes.
You can come to Him again and again and say, "God, I'm sorry for
(whatever I said or did)" and be sure He will forgive you.

---

*Dear God, I messed up today. I'm sorry for
_____. Please forgive me. Amen.*

I FORGIVE—ME!

He has taken our sins from us as far as the east is from the west.

PSALM 103:12

Have you read the Winnie-the-Pooh books? If you have, you know the character Eeyore. He's the little gray donkey who spends all his time worrying. Eeyore isn't a happy donkey. He carries around inside his heart all kinds of unhappy thoughts. If Eeyore messed up and made a mistake, he would probably keep thinking about that mistake. Even after he had been forgiven, he would walk around with his head hung low, feeling ashamed. When you mess up, you don't have to be like Eeyore. Once you've asked God for forgiveness, you can forgive yourself too. God took your sin away, and now you can let it go. God's forgiveness is a wonderful thing. It washes away your guilt and shame so you can feel happy again.

Dear God, I feel ashamed of what I did. Even though You've forgiven me, I still feel guilty. Please help me to feel happy again. Amen.

I FORGIVE—YOU!

Then Peter came to Jesus and said, "Lord, how many times may my brother sin against me and I forgive him, up to seven times?" Jesus said to him, "I tell you, not seven times but seventy times seven!"

MATTHEW 18:21–22

One of Jesus' helpers, Peter, asked Jesus how many times he had to forgive someone for treating him badly. "Up to seven times?" Peter guessed. Jesus' answer might have surprised Peter. He said, "Not seven times, but seventy times seven!" Can you do the math? 70 x 7 = 490. Jesus was teaching Peter that he must forgive others all the time. Forgiveness doesn't mean we allow people to continue to treat us badly. It means we forgive them inside our hearts. Forgiving others might not be easy, but we can ask God for help. We can ask Him to deal with what the other person did and then show us what to do.

Dear God, please help me to forgive _____. Show me what to do when someone treats me unfairly. Amen.

GRACE

Try to understand other people. Forgive each other.
If you have something against someone, forgive
him. That is the way the Lord forgave you.

COLOSSIANS 3:13

Your friend said something that hurt your feelings, and now you're angry. Maybe you want to get back at him by hurting his feelings too. Stop, and think about it. Try to understand why your friend said what he did. Was he trying to be mean, or did he just mess up? We all say and do things we feel sorry for. Even best friends mess up and quarrel sometimes. The word *grace* means to treat others well even when they treat us badly. Maybe a little grace from you would help heal how you feel about your friend. You can show grace by being forgiving and kind, and by treating your friend the way you want to be treated. Even if it's hard, try to be forgiving toward your friend the way God is forgiving toward you.

Dear God, my feelings are hurt, and I'm angry with
_____. Help me to let go of my bad feelings and show
some grace to the one who hurt me. Amen.

I MISUNDERSTOOD

*Don't jump to conclusions—there may be a perfectly
good explanation for what you just saw.*

PROVERBS 25:8 MSG

Imagine you're on a camping trip with your dad. It's night and it's dark. You wake up from a sound sleep and you see a shadowy figure entering the tent. You gasp! For a split second you feel afraid. Then you hear Dad's voice saying, "It's okay. It's just me." Things aren't always as they appear, and it can be easy to jump to conclusions. The same is true in relationships. You might see and hear things and misunderstand. If you see or hear something you are unsure of, look for the facts. Ask the person if what you saw or heard was true. If it's something dangerous or scary, tell a trusted adult. Friends sometimes have misunderstandings. If you aren't sure whether your friend meant to hurt you with her actions or words, ask. Good friends tell each other the truth. They tell each other when they don't understand.

---

*Dear God, things aren't always what they seem.
If I'm confused about someone's actions or words,
lead me to find out the truth. Amen.*

MERCY

"You must have loving-kindness just as
your Father has loving-kindness."
LUKE 6:36

It's one of those days when your little brother is being a real pain. You're almost done with your homework, and if he would just stop bugging you, you could be finished and outside with your friends. You've had enough of his interruptions. You say to him, "You're so irritating! Go away. Leave me alone!" Do you think you've hurt his feelings? Do you care? Many times younger siblings don't mean to be a pain. They want your attention, to be cared for, and to feel loved. There is something called "mercy." It means treating others with loving-kindness. When Jesus lived on earth, crowds followed Him around wanting His time and attention. Sometimes He wished to be left alone, but Jesus was always gentle with others and kind. Practice showing mercy to those who irritate you. Do your best to be understanding and patient.

Dear Jesus, there were times when You wanted to be alone,
but You were never harsh or scolded those who wanted
Your attention. Teach me to be more like You. Amen.

PATIENCE

Be completely humble and gentle; be patient,
bearing with one another in love.

EPHESIANS 4:2 NIV

If your teacher said, "Define the word *patience*," how would you answer? Patience means accepting that you have to wait, and then waiting without getting upset or angry. Waiting can be hard, especially when someone else has control over where you want to go and when you'll get there. Have you been irritated with your parents when you wanted to go somewhere and they told you to wait? You can learn to be patient by doing your best to let go of those irritated feelings and saying to yourself, "It's going to be okay." Sometimes just saying those words "It's going to be okay" is enough to help you calm down and make waiting easier. Patience helps you get along better with others too. Recognizing that family members and friends are busy and have their own things to take care of can help you become more caring, understanding, and kind.

Dear God, I don't like to wait. Will You help me learn
patience so waiting will be easier? Amen.

I UNDERSTAND

So comfort each other and make each other
strong as you are already doing.

1 THESSALONIANS 5:11

Your brother storms through the front door and throws his baseball glove on the kitchen table. "What's the matter?" you ask. "I messed up!" he answers. "The bases were loaded, the catcher threw the ball to me, and I didn't catch it. All the runners made it home, and we lost the game." You reply, "Wow, you really did mess up." How do you think your answer made your brother feel? A better answer would have been, "I know how that feels. I understand that you're disappointed. What can I do to help you feel better?" The Bible reminds us to comfort one another. We do that by being understanding and showing we care. Maybe you know someone who could use a little understanding today. What can you do to help?

Dear God, when someone is having a bad day,
remind me to be understanding of how they must
feel. Help me to show that I care. Amen.

WATCH YOUR WORDS

Let the words of my mouth and the thoughts
of my heart be pleasing in Your eyes, O Lord,
my Rock and the One Who saves me.

PSALM 19:14

The words you choose are important. They can help others feel good about themselves, or they can tear others down. How would you feel if someone said, "You can't do anything right" or "You're so weird"? Words like that can hurt. They can knock down a person's confidence. It's important to build people up by choosing good words. Saying things like "You tried hard and did your best" or "You're an awesome friend" will go a long way in helping others feel good about themselves. Remember to think before you speak. The Bible reminds us to use words that are pleasing to God. If they are pleasing to God, they will be pleasing to others too.

Dear God, forgive me for any words I've used that
might have hurt others. Please remind me to use words
that are encouraging, caring, and kind. Amen.

GENTLE AND KIND

They must not speak bad of anyone, and they must not argue. They should be gentle and kind to all people.

TITUS 3:2

One of Jesus' followers, a man named Paul, wrote a letter to Titus, his missionary friend. In his letter, Paul told his friend how Christians—those who believe in and follow Jesus—should speak to one another. Paul said they should do their best not to say bad things about anyone or argue, and they should be gentle and kind to everyone. Can you think of some examples of what it means to speak badly of someone? Maybe you said lying about others, criticizing them, or saying other unpleasant things. Saying bad things about others doesn't only hurt them; it makes God sad too. Speaking badly about others can cause arguments and lead people not to get along. When we are kind with our words and with one another, we help make the world a better place.

Dear God, sometimes I mess up and say things that are not so nice. Guide me to only speak well of others. Amen.

HOW TO AVOID AN ARGUMENT

A gentle answer turns away anger, but a sharp word causes anger.

PROVERBS 15:1

Imagine you just got home from school and you're hungry. In the kitchen, you find a plate with one big, fudgy brownie. It's yours! But just then your little sister runs into the room and sees you about to take it. She grabs the brownie and says, "Mine!" What would you say to her? You have a split second to choose your words. You could grab the brownie out of her hand and say, "I saw it first!" or you could say something like "Let's share it." A gentle answer can stop an argument before it begins, but a sharp answer usually causes anger. The next time you think a disagreement is about to happen, try a gentle answer. Put Proverbs 15:1 to the test. See if it prevents a quarrel.

Dear God, the Bible is filled with good advice. I learned from Proverbs 15:1 how I might avoid an argument. Now I can put what I've learned into action. Amen.

LIES HURT

A man who tells a lie against his neighbor is like
a heavy stick or a sword or a sharp arrow.

PROVERBS 25:18

The Bible says telling lies about someone is like hitting them with a heavy stick, a sword, or a sharp arrow. In other words, lies hurt! A lie doesn't hurt the body, but it does a lot of damage to a person's feelings. If someone lies and says you did something you didn't do, it could ruin your reputation—the opinion others have of you. When someone tells many lies, they risk not being trusted. There are no big lies or little lies. A lie is a lie, and telling a lie is never okay, especially if the lie is meant to hurt someone, avoid being punished, or get what you want. Practice building a good reputation by always telling the truth.

Dear God, I want to be an all-the-time truth teller. If
ever I feel like telling a lie about someone or something,
please give me courage to tell the truth. Amen.

IF THE TRUTH HURTS

"Be honest in what you do. Do not lie to one another."
LEVITICUS 19:11

Imagine you and your parents attended your cousin's first piano recital. Your cousin is very young and just learning. The song he played wasn't one of your favorites, and he hit many wrong notes. It wasn't a great performance; still, your cousin thought it was. "Did you like my song?" he asks. If you told the truth, it would hurt his feelings. Do you think it would be okay to lie and say you liked his song? Lying isn't okay even if it's a little lie. Instead of hurting your cousin with the truth, you could say something positive about his performance like "You must have practiced really hard! I'm so proud of you." Before you speak, think about your words, and choose them wisely. What could you say to your uncle if he gave you a gift you didn't like? What could you say to your grandmother if she prepared a meal you didn't enjoy?

---

*Dear God, thank You for helping me to be wise
when choosing my words. Amen.*

BUT WHAT IF?

*"Be strong and have strength of heart. Do not be
afraid or shake with fear because of them. For the
Lord your God is the One Who goes with you. He will
be faithful to you. He will not leave you alone."*

DEUTERONOMY 31:6

There is one time when telling a lie might be okay: if you were in
danger and a lie would protect you from getting hurt. You won't
be punished for doing whatever you have to do to stay safe and be
okay. Talk with your parents about it. Hopefully, you won't ever find
yourself in a dangerous situation, but it's good to be prepared. And
if you were in danger, you wouldn't be alone. God would be there
with you. He promises never to leave you. Whatever were to happen,
you can trust God to help you be strong and stay safe.

---

*Dear God, if ever I feel in danger, I will remember that You are
with me. I know You love me, and I am safe with You. Amen.*

GOSSIP

A perverse person stirs up conflict, and a
gossip separates close friends.

PROVERBS 16:28 NIV

Suppose you are eating lunch with a friend and he says, "I heard Andrew's dad was fired from his job." Repeating information about someone's private life is gossip. Gossip usually includes information that is unkind or might not be true. Gossip is talking about someone behind their back. Andrew isn't with you at the lunch table, so he can't comment on what your friend said. That's not fair to Andrew, and it isn't okay. Gossip can hurt feelings, cause trouble, and ruin friendships. Do you think it would be okay to repeat what you heard about Andrew's dad?

Think about how you would feel if you were Andrew. When you hear gossip, you can stop it by saying something like, "I don't feel good talking about this."

Dear God, thank you for reminding me that it's not okay to spread rumors and talk about people behind their backs. If I hear gossip, help me to use the best words to stop it. Amen.

SWEAR WORDS

Watch your talk! No bad words should be coming
from your mouth. Say what is good. Your words
should help others grow as Christians.

EPHESIANS 4:29

God hears every word you say. You've learned to stay away from lies and conversations that include gossip or are unkind toward others. But what about swearing? Is that okay? The Bible says to watch your talk so no bad words come from your mouth. Swearing is disrespectful. If a friend were swearing and using God's or Jesus' name, would you start using that kind of language too? When someone uses God's name to swear, God hears, and He doesn't like it. God's name should only be used when you are talking respectfully about Him or to Him in prayer. When you watch the way you talk, you will be a good role model for others, and that pleases God.

Dear God, I will watch my words and especially never use
Your name in a disrespectful way. I want my words to be
respectful and good so they are like music to Your ears. Amen.

SCARY WORDS

You came near when I called You, and You said, "Do not be afraid!"
LAMENTATIONS 3:57

Sometimes we hear words that worry us. They lead us to believe the world is a big and scary place. News reporters speak of things like crime, accidents, war, hurricanes, floods, fires, and pandemics. While listening, you might begin to worry about your own safety and wonder, *What if that happens to me?* The truth is that almost always those scary things you hear about on the news won't happen to you. And if they were to happen, you know you can count on God for help. He has power over all those scary things. If you hear a reporter, or anyone else, say words that frighten you, talk with your parents about what you hear. God made this big and wonderful world for you to explore and enjoy. He doesn't want you to be afraid.

Dear God, almost every day there's scary stuff in the news. Help me not to think and worry about it. Remind me to focus on the good things. Amen.

ENCOURAGING WORDS

Therefore encourage one another with these words.

1 THESSALONIANS 4:18 NIV

Jesus encouraged us to care for one another. We can show we care by choosing words that encourage—words that lead others to believe that everything will be okay. Words matter. They can build people up or tear them down. Encouraging words are the best because they always build people up and make them feel good about themselves. Can you think of a time when someone encouraged you with their words? Maybe you were afraid to try something new and a parent or a friend encouraged you by saying, "You can do it!" or "Keep up the good work!" or "I'm so proud of you." Encouragement helps others to feel confident and able. Think of three things you could say to encourage someone. Keep those words inside your heart and ready. Do you know someone who needs some encouragement today?

Dear God, I want to be an encourager like Jesus.
Open my eyes to those who need encouragement.
Then give me the right words to say. Amen.

I DON'T KNOW WHAT TO SAY

Moses said to the Lord, "Lord, I am not a man of words. . . .
I am slow in talking and it is difficult for me to speak."
EXODUS 4:10

God told His friend Moses to deliver an important message to the Egyptian pharaoh, or king. The thought of speaking to such a powerful man made Moses afraid. *This is not okay,* Moses thought. God saw how worried Moses was, so He sent Moses' brother, Aaron, to help. God said, "I will help you both with your words. Aaron will speak to the people for you" (see Exodus 4:15–16). So Aaron and Moses went together to speak to Pharaoh. There might be a time when you need help talking with someone about something important. Ask God to give you wisdom to choose the best words. If you aren't sure what to say, ask a parent or other trusted adult for advice. Maybe the two of you can talk with that person together.

Dear God, when I don't know what to say, please send me a
helper, someone who can help me choose the right words. Amen.

GOD'S WORD

*No part of the Holy Writings was ever made up by
any man. No part of the Holy Writings came long ago
because of what man wanted to write. But holy men who
belonged to God spoke what the Holy Spirit told them.*

2 PETER 1:20–21

The Bible is called "God's Word." Every word was inspired by God. That means the thoughts written down by the Bible's authors came from God. As you read your Bible, you will grow in wisdom. You will learn that God knows everything, He has all the answers, He is in control of everything, He is more powerful than anything worrisome or scary, He loves you, and He promises to help you and make you strong. When you read the Bible and think about its words, You can imagine God speaking to you. Keep His words inside your heart. When you feel worried or afraid, you can remember God's words and know that everything will be okay.

---

*Dear God, when I read the Bible, I will remember it is You
speaking to me. I will keep Your words inside my heart. Amen.*

SHHH!

There is a time. . .to be quiet, and a time to speak.

ECCLESIASTES 3:7

Imagine that your family is on a road trip. Your little brother is bored riding in the car, and he's being obnoxious, doing and saying things to irritate you. Would it be a good time to speak up and tell him to stop? If your words might start an argument, it might be best not to speak. Think about times when it might be good to stay silent. Should you be quiet if your words might hurt someone? Would it be right to repeat something you heard about someone, especially if you didn't see it happen, hear it said, or can't be sure that it's true? The Bible says there is a time for everything, a time to be quiet and a time to speak. Get in the habit of thinking about your words. If you feel like saying angry or hurtful words or repeating gossip, choose silence instead.

Dear God, guide me. Teach me to know when to
stay silent and when to speak. Amen.

FACE THOSE FIRSTS!

*"Have I not told you? Be strong and have strength
of heart! Do not be afraid or lose faith. For the Lord
your God is with you anywhere you go."*
JOSHUA 1:9

You might feel butterflies in your stomach when you do something for the first time. It could be the first day at a new school, the first time you're away from your parents for a while, the first time you perform for an audience, the first time you ride in an airplane, or some other new experience. From the day you were born, you've been doing things for the first time. Some firsts were easy; others took courage. Each first you accomplished helped you gain confidence so you could tackle the next one without being so afraid. God is with you wherever you go. He will give you courage to face those firsts and know that everything will be all right. Is there something you would like to try for the first time? Ask God to do it with you.

Dear God, I would like to try _____. Will You do it with me? Amen.

SATAN'S TRAP

Don't fall into the trap of being a coward—
trust the LORD, and you will be safe.
PROVERBS 29:25 CEV

Satan is God's archenemy—God's worst enemy. Satan doesn't like it when people love God and try to do what's right, so he works very hard at making them feel as if things aren't okay. Satan whispers words inside our hearts, telling us we aren't good enough, strong enough, or courageous enough, along with other lies. At the same time, God is telling us we *are* good enough, strong enough, and courageous enough. God is way more powerful than His enemy, Satan, and He doesn't want us to fall into the enemy's trap. So if you hear Satan saying you can't do something, push his words away! Listen to God instead. God will always encourage you. When you trust Him, you will feel safe knowing God is the one who gives you power and strength to conquer all your fears.

Dear God, help me learn to recognize Your voice inside
my heart. Give me courage to stand up to fear. Amen.

NEW SCHOOL

"Do not be afraid, just believe."

MARK 5:36

Maybe you've been here: your family moved in the middle of a school year, and you had to start at a new school. It's always a little scary facing the first day of a new school year, but if you have to start school after all the other kids were there awhile, your fear can kick into high gear. Some scary firsts can't be avoided. You just have to gather all your strength and dig in. God wants you to know you're not going into it alone. He says, "Don't be afraid, just believe." Believe in Him and all His power to help you. God will walk into that school with you; and if you try, you can feel Him giving you courage to face the first day in an unfamiliar place filled with people you don't know. Trust Him. Soon that new school will be your school, and you'll feel comfortable there.

Dear God, I will trust in You and believe in
Your power to help me. Amen.

FITTING IN

We all have different gifts that God has given to
us by His loving-favor. We are to use them.

ROMANS 12:6

If you struggle fitting in at a new school, try using the gifts God gave you. When you were born, God put inside you all kinds of things you are good at—special skills and talents. Maybe you are good at playing sports, creating art, dancing, making music, acting, writing, building things, playing chess, or something else. Look for kids at your new school who are good at those same things. Get involved in groups and clubs that interest you. If God put it in your heart to be a helper, seek out people who could use your help and also those who are helping others. Put your great ideas to work. List five things you are good at. When you reach out to those who share your skills and talents, you're sure to make some awesome new friends.

Dear God, open my eyes to my talents and skills
and help me put them to use. Amen.

WHO, WHAT, WHERE, WHEN, WHY?

Two are better than one, because they
have good pay for their work.

ECCLESIASTES 4:9

The Bible says, "Two are better than one." Two friends are good, but three friends, four friends, five friends, six. . .are even better. How can you find friends with whom you have things in common? By asking questions. When you meet someone new, show you're interested in getting to know that person. You could ask if they like something you enjoy. For example, you could ask, "Do you play soccer?" or "What activities do you do after school?" or "How many brothers and sisters do you have?" or even "Do you like the food in our cafeteria?" When you ask a question, follow it up by being a good listener. Give the other person plenty of time to talk and ask you questions too.

Dear God, please lead me to good friends, those who have things in common with me and who behave in ways that please You. Amen.

CLIQUES

*My Christian brothers, our Lord Jesus Christ is the Lord
of shining-greatness. Since your trust is in Him, do not
look on one person as more important than another.*

JAMES 2:1

A clique is a group of friends who leave other kids out of their group on purpose. Not always, but sometimes, kids in a clique make fun of other kids and are even mean to them. That's not okay! If ever you're left out of a clique, whatever you do, don't blame yourself. You don't need friends who see themselves as more important than you. Instead, focus on finding friends who are more like yourself. Look for friends not just at school, but at church, family gatherings—everywhere. Invite a new friend to hang out with you and to participate in some of your family activities at church or elsewhere. God loves it when you welcome new friends into your life, especially those who make others feel valued.

---

*Dear God, it hurts to feel left out. Help me find friends
who are welcoming, caring, and kind. Amen.*

PEER PRESSURE

"Do not follow many people in doing wrong."
EXODUS 23:2

There is an ancient myth about lemmings, a type of small rodent, running after one another into danger. According to the myth, one by one they jump off a cliff and drown in the sea. It's only a myth, but the idea of hundreds of furry little mouse-like creatures following one another into danger is something to remember. It's like what humans do when they give in to peer pressure. Following the crowd is never a good idea when the crowd is leading you toward something dangerous or wrong. If the kids you hang around with are heading in the wrong direction, don't join in or be afraid to turn around. God has given you wisdom to know the difference between right and wrong. Follow your heart and do what's right. Take it one step further. Be a role model and lead your friends in the right direction.

Dear God, if my friends are going the wrong way, remind me not to follow. Help me lead them toward doing what's right. Amen.

UNHEALTHY HABITS

"Do not let us be tempted, but keep us from sin."

MATTHEW 6:13

You might know of kids in your school or an older sibling's school who have experimented with drugs, alcohol, cigarettes, and other unhealthy things. These things aren't only unhealthy; they can be dangerous. If you know of someone who is using drugs or alcohol or trying to get other kids to try, the right thing to do is tell a trusted adult. You can do it privately. Tell them what you saw or what you know to be true. Your goal isn't to get anyone in trouble or to spread gossip; it's to get them out of danger. If someone tries to get you to try those things, you should say no. Pray for those who are engaging in unhealthy activities. Ask God to keep them away from trouble.

Dear God, when You see kids trying drugs, alcohol, and other dangerous things, please lead them to stop. I want them to follow You and do what's healthy and good. Amen.

WHAT MAKES A GOOD FRIEND?

*Do not let anyone fool you. Bad people can make
those who want to live good become bad.*

1 CORINTHIANS 15:33

Imagine that your teacher asked you to write an essay about what makes a good friend. Before you write, you would have to consider all those things you like in a friend. Maybe you would think about your best friends and why you like them. Good friends are caring, kind, truthful, trustworthy, fun to be with, patient, understanding, and forgiving. Can you add more to the list? Good friends stand up for one another, encourage one another, and pray for one another. Most of all, they help one another do what's right. You are a good friend. What do you think others might write in their essay about you? Jesus is the best of friends. What would you write if your essay was about Him?

---

*Dear Jesus, when I read about You in the Bible,
I see what it means to be a good friend. I'm trying
every day to become more like You. Amen.*

MY OWN SPECIAL STYLE

But now, O Lord, You are our Father. We are the clay, and You are our pot maker. All of us are the work of Your hand.

ISAIAH 64:8

Have you ever watched someone create a painting or sculpture? No two works of art are alike. Each artist has a special style. You have your own special style too. There isn't another person on the planet who is exactly like you nor will there ever be. This is your time to show the world who you are and what you can do. God made you to be unique—one of a kind. Maybe you like to dress differently from the other kids in school, or maybe you are different on the inside in ways that can't be seen. Don't hide from the world because you are different. Instead, celebrate your differences and allow them to shine.

Dear God, sometimes I'm a little nervous to show the world the real me. Help me to put my real self out there. I want to show others the amazing person You made me to be. Amen.

DISABILITIES

*His followers asked Him, "Teacher, whose sin made this man
to be born blind? Was it the sin of this man or the sin of his
parents?" Jesus answered, "The sin of this man or the sin
of his parents did not make him to be born blind. He was
born blind so the work of God would be seen in him."*

JOHN 9:2–3

God often uses disabilities to show the world that His work is always
perfect. For example, Joni Eareckson Tada became paralyzed in a
diving accident, but that didn't stop God from helping her accomplish great things. She became famous for painting pictures using
a brush held in her teeth. Fame led Joni to write a book, and that
book led to her introducing people to Jesus and His love for them.
Today Joni hosts a Christian radio show. She helps people with disabilities to be treated fairly and to be given the same opportunities
everyone else has. When you see someone with a disability, look for
God working through them, leading them to do amazing things.

---

*Dear God, I see You working through everyone
who puts their faith in You. Amen.*

I'M NOT BOSSY!

As much as you can, live in peace with all men.
ROMANS 12:18

How would you feel if your friend said, "You shouldn't style your hair that way. Let me show you how to do it." Or what if your friend didn't like the movie you chose, took the remote from your hand, and said, "Here, let me choose the movie"? Bossy people often want something done their way, and they want others to do it their way too. That's no fun! Friends get along better when they allow each other to do things differently. Sometimes that means taking turns doing what the other wants or compromising, with each person giving up a little and agreeing on something they both will enjoy. Bossing people around is never good. If you find yourself feeling a little bossy, flip that feeling upside down. Practice compromising and taking turns.

Dear God, thank You for reminding me to think about what others might want to do. Being a good friend means taking turns, compromising, and sharing. Amen.

DO YOU REALLY WANT THAT FRIEND?

"Whoever has nothing to do with you, has nothing to do with Me."
LUKE 10:16

You did your best to be a good friend. But what if, as hard as you tried, someone didn't want to be your friend? Rejection hurts. You could help the hurt go away by asking yourself, "Do I really want to be friends with someone who is unkind to me?" You deserve better. God says you are awesome just as you are. He wants you to have friends who think you are totally awesome too. Jesus told His followers, "Whoever has nothing to do with you, has nothing to do with Me." Jesus wanted His friends to be with those who respected, accepted, and behaved toward them in the loving ways Jesus did. Think about who you really want to be friends with and choose your friends wisely.

Dear Jesus, if someone doesn't want to be my friend, I will remember that You want me to have friends who love and respect me. Amen.

THE FAVORITE TEACHER

"The follower is not more important than his teacher.
But everyone who learns well will be like his teacher."

LUKE 6:40

Do you have a favorite teacher? Why is he or she your favorite? Maybe you answered, "Because my teacher is nice," or said that your teacher is funny or kind. Those are great answers. But think about what you've learned from your teacher. Teachers help you have confidence in your abilities, encourage you to do your best, and guide you toward being patient. They help you understand that if you fail at something you shouldn't give up but keep on trying. Teachers help you get better at things you are good at, and they help you improve on those things you're not so good at. A good teacher is trustworthy and someone you can confide in, especially if someone at school is mean to you or if something dangerous is going on. Teachers need to feel appreciated just like everyone else, so remember to thank your teachers for all they do.

Dear God, thank You for my teachers.
Bless all their hard work. Amen.

THE NOT-SO-FAVORITE TEACHER

Obey your leaders and do what they say. They keep watch over your souls. They have to tell God what they have done. They should have joy in this and not be sad. If they are sad, it is no help to you.

HEBREWS 13:17

Sometimes people don't get along because their personalities are so opposite. That can be true about teachers and their students. There might be something about a teacher you don't like. But that doesn't mean you shouldn't be respectful of your teacher. The Bible says, "Obey your leaders, and do what they say." Remind yourself that no one is perfect—not even teachers. Then do your best to overlook your teacher's flaws. Sometimes, though, you might have an issue with a teacher that is more than just your personalities not fitting together. If you feel uncomfortable with a teacher or believe you are being treated unfairly, tell a parent. Together decide what you might do to make the situation better.

Dear God, help me to be respectful of my teachers and everyone else, even when it's hard. Amen.

THE BEST TEACHER

Jesus said to them, "What I teach is not
Mine. It is from God Who sent Me."

JOHN 7:16

If someone asks you, "Who is the best teacher?" you can answer, "Jesus!" When He lived on earth, Jesus' followers called Him "Rabbi," which means "teacher." Jesus is the best teacher because everything He taught came directly from God. Every word Jesus spoke, everything He taught about the right way to live, came from God. Sometimes Jesus was direct when He taught. He told people exactly what they should do. Other times Jesus told stories called "parables." They were designed to make people think. You can learn what Jesus taught by reading the Bible. The first four books of the New Testament (Matthew, Mark, Luke, and John) are all about Jesus. Read them and learn from Jesus what God says about being respectful and living right.

Dear Jesus, I want You to be my teacher. I want to
learn from You how to get along well with others
and live in ways that please God. Amen.

TRYING TOO HARD

I am not trying to please people. I want to please God.
GALATIANS 1:10 CEV

It's always good to work hard and try your best, but did you know that sometimes you can try too hard? Maybe math or another school subject is giving you trouble. You're trying so hard to get it right that you begin to feel sick. You feel disappointed in yourself, and you worry that your teacher will be disappointed in you too. That's not okay! This is one of those times when you need to turn your thinking upside down. Be proud of yourself for doing your best, even if your best needs improvement. God sees how hard you're trying, and He is proud of you. Give yourself a break from your work. Then give it another try. And never be afraid to ask for help. Your teacher sees how hard you're trying. Instead of being disappointed in you, he or she wants you to feel good about yourself and what you can do.

Dear God, help me, please, not to be so hard on myself. Amen.

WHEN PARENTS MESS UP

Parents, don't be hard on your children.
If you are, they might give up.
COLOSSIANS 3:21 CEV

News flash: parents aren't perfect! Moms and dads mess up sometimes, just like you do. They say and do things that later they're sorry for. A bad day at work or some other problem can lead to a crabby parent at the dinner table. If that crabby parent uses words or acts in ways that are less than calm or kind, you might worry that it's because of something you've done. It's not! Most of the time, it's best just to give a crabby mom or dad some space. Don't argue or do something that will add to their already bad day. When your parent is calm again, maybe the two of you can talk about why their bad mood upset you. Your parents love you, and they don't want their problems to become yours.

Dear God, my parents get upset sometimes, and their
bad moods worry me. Please help my mom and dad to
work out their problems and stay calm. Amen.

GOD UNDERSTANDS

*But You, O Lord, are a God full of love and pity. You are
slow to anger and rich in loving-kindness and truth.*

PSALM 86:15

Imagine you messed up big-time. You did something you knew
was wrong, and God saw the whole thing. Your parents are
disappointed—not in you, but in what you chose to do. The only
word that can describe how you feel is *guilty*. Maybe you're worried
that God is so upset by what He saw that He won't want to hear
from you. Nothing could be further from the truth. God loves you.
He understands you aren't perfect and—get this—He expects you
to mess up! All humans mess up sometimes, and when they come
to God and say they're sorry, God always forgives them. Go to God
and pray. He already knows you feel guilty. If you ask Him to forgive
you, He will wipe from His memory whatever He saw you do.

---

*Dear God, I'm embarrassed that You saw what I did. Thank You
for forgiving me and choosing to forget what I've done. Amen.*

HOMEWORK OVERLOAD

Whatever work you do, do it with all your heart.
Do it for the Lord and not for men.

COLOSSIANS 3:23

English, language arts, math, science, social studies—they all come with homework, and sometimes too much homework. All the other stuff you have to get done adds to the homework overload. Something has to give! So what will you do? You could rush through your homework and not do it well. You could avoid doing it altogether. Or you could dig in, do your best, and get it done. Which would you choose? The Bible provides one way to look at a homework overload. It says that whatever you do, do it as if you were doing it for God, and do it with all your heart. Imagine if God had given you your homework assignments today and said, "Will you do your best for Me?" How would you answer Him?

Dear God, whenever it feels like I have too much work or the work is too hard, remind me that everything I do, I do for You. Amen.

STUDY AND LEARN

I have taught you in the way of wisdom. I have led
you on the right paths. . . . Take hold of teaching.
Do not let go. Watch over her, for she is your life.

PROVERBS 4:11, 13

God wants you to study and learn so you will grow in wisdom. Becoming wise doesn't just happen. It takes a lot of studying and hard work. Learning is like building a skyscraper. First, you build the ground floor. Then you work your way up. Each new floor adds something new and helps make the building stronger. Think about the ways you've built on what you've already learned. For example, first you learned letters, then you learned to put them together to make words. You put the words together to make sentences, and then you put sentences together to write stories, poems, and essays. Learning never ends. When you put your learning to use every day the wiser you will become.

Dear God, remind me to study hard and learn my
lessons well. Lead me toward wisdom. Amen.

LIFE LESSONS

*I forget everything that is behind me and look
forward to that which is ahead of me.*

PHILIPPIANS 3:13

Can you think of a time when a mistake taught you a life lesson? A life lesson is a piece of wisdom you will carry with you for the rest of your life. Maybe you thought you had nothing in common with the new kid in class, so you didn't make an effort to be his friend. Later you discovered the two of you have a lot in common. You could learn from that not to be quick to judge others. Or maybe in a moment of anger you said something mean to your sister that made her cry. That mistake could teach you to be more understanding and kind. The best thing about life lessons is that they help you put the mistake in the past and learn to do better in the future.

*Dear God, help me to handle my mistakes in a good
way. Guide me to learn from them. Amen.*

A TIME FOR EVERYTHING

*There is a special time for everything. There is a time
for everything that happens under heaven.*

ECCLESIASTES 3:1

Mom says, "Write it on the calendar." You have so much stuff going on in your life, it's easy to forget what you need to do and when. If you don't write it down, you and your parents might find yourselves dashing around at the last minute trying to get you where you have to go and do what you have to do. A schedule is important. It keeps life moving along smoothly, and that leads to less stress and fewer arguments at home. Take some time with your parents to create a schedule together. Then stick to it. Plan a block of time every day to do homework and chores. Plug in some time for fun. And don't forget to set aside quiet time to pray and be alone with God.

---

*Dear God, I need to become more organized. Lead
my parents and me to create a schedule that will
work for us. Then help us stick to it. Amen.*

A PLACE FOR EVERYTHING

All things should be done in the right way, one after the other.

1 CORINTHIANS 14:40

"Where's my backpack?" "Has anyone seen my jacket?" "I lost my homework!" "I can't find my shoes." If you're always losing things and wasting time looking for them, maybe it's time to get organized. A messy room leads to lost stuff, and lost stuff leads to you feeling frustrated, and you feeling frustrated leads to Mom and Dad feeling frustrated too. You can avoid all that frustration by keeping your space organized and clean. If you spend just a few minutes each day picking up your stuff and putting it away, you can avoid those marathon room cleaning sessions you hate. First Corinthians 14:40 says all things should be done in the right way. Combine that with a scripture you've already learned: "Whatever work you do. . .Do it for the Lord" (Colossians 3:23). Your work will be lighter when you do it for Him.

Dear God, thank You for reminding me to keep things neat and clean. I'll do my best to do better. Amen.

A JUGGLING ACT

Have you found honey? Eat only what you need,
or you may become filled with it and spit it up.

PROVERBS 25:16

There are so many fun things to do, it might be hard to choose. If you wanted, you could cram tons of activities into your after-school schedule, enough to take up all your time. Playing sports, music or dance lessons, being in the school play, church youth group activities, clubs, hobbies, volunteering—they're all fun, but they also can become too much. You can create a schedule so busy it turns into a juggling act! Have you ever seen a juggler try to juggle too many things and they all fall down? Something similar can happen when you cram too much into your schedule—it can all come crashing down in the form of stress and not enjoying those fun things as much. Be wise with your time. You don't have to do everything at once. Prioritize those things you love the most, and let the others go.

Dear God, help me to prioritize and choose what's best. Amen.

TESTS AND EXAMS

"The Lord is the One Who goes before you. He will be with you. He will be faithful to you and will not leave you alone. Do not be afraid or troubled."

DEUTERONOMY 31:8

Imagine that your teacher says, "Remember, there's a test tomorrow. I expect all of you to do well." Her words make your heart flip-flop. You feel nervous every time there's a test. You want to do well and get a perfect grade. You begin to worry, saying to yourself, *What if I fail?* But if you're prepared—and you probably are—you don't have to feel worried. You've studied the material, asked for help if you didn't understand, and you're ready. Even so, you still feel unsettled. You can chase those jitters away by remembering you aren't taking that test alone. God will be with you. He will help you relax and do your best. Learn to trust God and give your worries to Him. He will never let you down.

Dear God, take my worries and calm me down. I put my trust in You. Amen.

I DID MY BEST

Everyone who runs in a race does many things so his body will be strong. He does it to get a crown that will soon be worth nothing, but we work for a crown that will last forever.

1 CORINTHIANS 9:25

Jesus' follower Paul said that many people run in a race, but only one wins. He said to get in shape and do your best. But if you lose, remember that winning isn't as important as knowing that God is pleased with you for trying. Paul reminded his friends that everything they do, they should do for God. If you do your best, that pleases God. If you are a good sport when you lose, that pleases God too. Whether it's a race or a test, God wants you to do your best for Him and then be okay with yourself and with others if you fail. Think about it: Do you give yourself credit for trying, or do you beat yourself up for losing?

Dear God, win or lose, it's enough that I did my best. Amen.

POWER BOOST

The LORD gives strength to those who are weary. Even young people get tired, then stumble and fall. But those who trust the LORD will find new strength. They will be strong like eagles soaring upward on wings; they will walk and run without getting tired.

ISAIAH 40:29–31 CEV

You tried, you failed, and you kept trying. Now you're tired. You feel discouraged and want to give up. You need a power boost, and God is ready to give you one! The Bible is filled with God's promises. They were His promises when the Bible was written, and they are still His promises today. If you put your trust in God, He promises to give you strength when you're weary. He will help you find renewed energy to keep trying and doing your best. When you feel tired and discouraged, ask God to give you a power boost. Then trust that He will.

Dear God, I'm tired, discouraged, and grumpy. I've done my best, and I feel like giving up. I need a power boost, please. Amen.

GRADES

Everyone should look at himself and see how he does his
own work. Then he can be happy in what he has done.
He should not compare himself with his neighbor.

GALATIANS 6:4

You've taken the exam, and your teacher is passing the graded tests back to the class. You look at your paper and discover you have three answers wrong. You wonder how your grade measures up with your friend's. You lean toward her and whisper, "What did you get?" If your friend got a better grade, would it make you upset with yourself for not doing better? If your friend got a worse grade, would that make you feel better about yours? Galatians 6:4 reminds you not to compare your work with others' work. Give yourself credit for trying hard and doing your best work. If your grade wasn't as good as you expected, tell yourself that next time you'll do even better.

Dear God, I had hoped for a better grade on the
test, but I'm not giving up or getting upset with
myself. Maybe next time I'll do better. Amen.

I'M SO DISAPPOINTED

*Why are you sad, O my soul? Why have you
become troubled within me? Hope in God, for I
will yet praise Him, my help and my God.*

PSALM 42:11

Your basketball team is playing its archrival. It's an important game, and in the final minutes of the last period, the score is super close. You get the ball, dribble it, run down the court, and shoot for the basket. You miss the field goal, and that contributes to your team losing the game. You feel disappointed. You expected yourself to play better, and if you were going to miss the basket, why did it have to happen at the end of the game? We don't know why things happen, but when disappointments happen, the best place to go with them is to God. He loves you all the time, win or lose. God will help ease your disappointment and give you hope.

*Dear God, I'm so disappointed. I'm glad You love me and that I
can come and talk with You. Please help me to feel better. Amen.*

I DON'T GET IT

Where no counsel is, the people fall: but in the
multitude of counsellors there is safety.

PROVERBS 11:14 KJV

Are you shy about asking for help? Many kids are. Sometimes you might think everyone else understands math, science, grammar, and other school subjects. But there are plenty of kids who don't understand everything the teacher is trying to teach. It's okay to say, "I don't get it." The Bible tells stories of people who failed because they didn't seek wise counsel. If you don't understand something, there are people all around you who care about you and want to help: teachers, parents, an older sibling, even a friend. You shouldn't be embarrassed or afraid to ask. Think about it, if someone asked you for help, would you make fun of them or judge them for not understanding? No, you wouldn't. And neither will those who care for you.

Dear God, when there are things I don't understand,
please help me to be brave and ask for help. Amen.

I DON'T WANT TO!

I can do all things because Christ gives me the strength.

PHILIPPIANS 4:13

What if you don't want to do your homework, clean your room, do your chores, or go to school? What if you don't want to forgive a friend who hurt you, be nice to your sister, or obey your parents? Sometimes, it's okay to say no. ("No thanks. I'm not a fan of broccoli." "No thanks. I don't feel like playing a video game.") But there are times when you shouldn't say no. You have to do things like obey your parents and go to school. When you're faced with something you don't want to do, remember Jesus. He knew He had to give up His life so people could live in heaven someday. He didn't want to face that pain and suffering, but He did it. When there's something you don't want to do, ask Jesus to give you strength to get it done.

Dear Jesus, I don't feel like doing homework today, but I know I have to. Please give me the strength to do it. Amen.

BUDDIES

Then Aaron and Hur held up his hands, one on each side.

EXODUS 17:12

There's a story in the Bible about the Israelites' army fighting an enemy. God gave Moses, the Israelites' leader, a special stick to hold in his hands. When Moses held up his hands, Israel's side would be winning the war. But when Moses let down his hands, the other side's army would win. After a while, Moses got tired of holding up the stick in his hands. His friends, Aaron and Hur saw. They hurried over to Moses and told him to sit. Then they stood on either side of Moses and held up his hands. Moses' buddies saved the day—Israel won the war. It's good to have buddies who will rush to your side whenever you need help. Do you have friends like that? Look for friends who are buddies. Those kinds of friends are lifelong friends. They'll stay by your side, and they won't let you down.

Dear God, thank You for friends who help me,
care for me, and stand up for me. Amen.

SPEAK UP

Give all your worries to Him because He cares for you.

1 PETER 5:7

Some kids are quiet, and some kids aren't. There are kids who are first to raise a hand to answer the teacher's questions, and there are kids who would rather wait quietly to be called on. Which are you? If you prefer being quiet, that's okay. But there will be times when you have to use your voice. The Israelites' leader, Moses, was nervous to speak up, but God helped Moses overcome his feelings. The more Moses spoke to a group, the more his confidence grew. Moses became a great leader and someone people looked up to. He was no longer afraid to speak. If you worry about speaking up, give your worries to God. Ask Him to do for you what He did for Moses. Then raise your hand with confidence and answer the questions your teacher asks.

Dear God, I'm a little nervous to raise my hand or to speak in front of my class. Please help me the way you helped Moses. Amen.

JUDGING OTHERS

*"Do not say what is wrong in other people's lives.
Then other people will not say what is wrong in your
life. . . . When you say what is wrong in others, your
words will be used to say what is wrong in you."*

MATTHEW 7:1–2

Maybe you worry kids will make fun of you if you speak up and answer a question incorrectly. If that were to happen—and it probably won't—you should remember what Jesus said. People who say what's wrong with others don't see what's wrong with themselves. Jesus told us to love one another and be kind. If someone made fun of you, they would be doing exactly what Jesus said not to do. Instead of feeling embarrassed by their comments, say a silent prayer for them. Ask God to forgive them for being rude and unkind. Don't allow their comments to stop you from speaking up and doing your best.

Dear God, forgive those who say unkind things about me. Guide them nearer to You and teach them to be loving and kind. Amen.

NOBODY'S PERFECT

For all men have sinned and have missed
the shining-greatness of God.

ROMANS 3:23

Do you know someone who's perfect? Maybe there's someone you really admire, a person with all the qualities you want to have. You'd like to be perfect just like him or her. The truth is, the person you admire isn't perfect, and neither is anyone else. Only God is perfect. He has never made a mistake or messed up in any way, and He never will. It's good to try hard and do your best, but if you're constantly trying to be perfect or do perfect work, you'll only make yourself feel anxious. God expects you to be who you are, imperfections and all. It's okay not to be perfect. You don't have to live up to someone else's standards. You don't have to worry about being accepted by anyone other than God. He accepts you just for being you, the way you are right now.

Dear God, I expect too much from myself. Sometimes
I feel like I'm not good enough. Please help me
to accept myself just as I am. Amen.

WORRIED SICK

Search me, God, and know my heart;
test me and know my anxious thoughts.

PSALM 139:23 NIV

Worrying can make you sick. You might have headaches or stomachaches. You could have a racing heart, sweaty palms, and feel out of breath. You might even feel like throwing up. Feeling worried and sick at the same time can be scary. If you don't feel well, tell a parent, teacher, or other adult. If you discover that it's worry that is making you sick, remember that God knows your anxious thoughts, and He doesn't want you to worry. God is big and strong and more powerful than anything that frightens you. He is in control and aware of what is causing you to worry. Right now He wants you to know He is with you, so you don't need to be afraid. Practice giving your worries to God and trusting Him to keep you safe.

Dear God, sometimes I worry so much I feel sick. You
have power over everything I worry about. I know
You love me and will help me feel safe. Amen.

NEVER ALONE

Keep me safe as You would Your own eye.
Hide me in the shadow of Your wings.
PSALM 17:8

Being away from home can sometimes be scary. Your house and everything in it are familiar. You feel safe there because you trust your parents to watch over you and keep you safe. If you have to be away from home, someplace unfamiliar, you might miss your house and your parents. That can make you feel anxious. Think about this: your parents will never send you to a dangerous place. If they leave you in the care of other adults for a while, they know they can trust those adults to keep you safe. Being away from home can be fun, especially when it's a sleepover, at camp, a field trip, or a stay with Grandma and Grandpa. Wherever you go, you are never alone because God is with you. He will guard you and keep you safe.

Dear God, help me to feel safe, not only at home but
away from home with grown-ups I trust. Amen.

I HATE GYM CLASS!

I pray that you are doing well in every way. I pray that
your body is strong and well even as your soul is.

3 JOHN 1:2

Maybe you're a kid who enjoys sports with your friends, but you hate gym class. You worry that you might be last to be picked for a team, or you feel that your classmates are better than you at volleyball, gymnastics, or running a race. Maybe you feel uncomfortable changing clothes in front of the other kids. If gym class isn't a great place for you, think about why. Does something about it make you feel you aren't good enough? Remember that God says you are good enough just as you are. If gym class is a problem for some other reason, talk with your parents about it. See if together you can come up with ideas to help you feel more comfortable.

Dear God, will You guide me to feeling more comfortable
in gym class? I know exercise is important to
keep my body healthy and strong. Amen.

A MATTER OF TASTE

*God said, "See, I have given you every plant
that gives seeds. . .and every tree that has
fruit. . . . They will be food for you."*

GENESIS 1:29

Maybe your taste in food is different from your friend's. In your school lunch bag, there's a ham sandwich, an apple, and a granola bar. Your friend's lunch has a few dates and a pita wrap filled with hummus, olives, tomatoes, and mint. How do you react when someone eats something you don't like or food unfamiliar to you? God, the Creator, made all kinds of food for us to enjoy, and it's fun to try a little of everything. In the Bible, John the Baptist ate locusts and honey—not that you would want to eat locusts. But understand it's good to try new things. If you'll taste something new and try some of the food your friends enjoy, you might just discover you like it!

---

*Dear God, give me courage to try some of the foods I think I
won't like. I won't know if I like them unless I try. Amen.*

GOD IS MY SAFE PLACE

The Lord also keeps safe those who suffer.
He is a safe place in times of trouble.

PSALM 9:9

When you hear about bad things happening in a school or to kids who are around your age, you might worry, *Could that happen to me?* God doesn't want worry to fill your mind with frightening or unhappy thoughts. He promises to be your safe place in times of trouble. If ever you were in danger, you could be sure God is with you. If you were hurt, God would be there at your side. If you were afraid, you could pray and ask God to calm you. If you were lost, God would find you. When scary thoughts fill your head, replace them with thoughts about God. Remember His promises. Listen for His words inside your heart. God is the one you can run to in times of trouble. You can trust in Him for help.

Dear God, help me replace any scary thoughts with
thoughts about You. You are my safe place. Wherever
I go, whatever I do, You are with me. Amen.

CHASE THOSE THOUGHTS AWAY

"When the earth and all its people shake,
it is I Who will hold it together."

PSALM 75:3

Scary thoughts can pile up, one on another. They can make you shiver and shake. Scary thoughts can make you freeze right where you are and not take one more step, or they can make you want to run away as fast as you can. If you allow one scary thought to take up space in your head, it will open the door to others. Don't allow it! You have power over those scary thoughts. You can tell them to go away because God rules the universe. Nothing is bigger or more powerful than God. When His people shiver and shake with fear, God goes to war with whatever makes them afraid—and God always wins. Whatever scary thought comes into your head, God's got it, and He's already working on it. So chase those thoughts away! You don't have to worry or be afraid.

Dear God, I've let worries pile up inside me. Please take them away from me. I don't want anything to do with them. Amen.

AN ARMY OF ANGELS

For He will tell His angels to care for you
and keep you in all your ways.

PSALM 91:11

If ever you find yourself in danger, God has a whole army of angels ready to help. He promises to send angels to protect you. Angels are helpers sent from heaven and are most often invisible. You won't see them, but they are all around. If angels see trouble coming your way, they often stop it before you even know. People can be like angels too. God uses people the way He uses angels. He puts it in people's thoughts to help. You might have heard stories of people who rushed in to save someone from drowning or from a burning building. Sometimes we say about their heroic acts, "They were angels in disguise." God's helpers are everywhere. When you are in trouble, all you have to do is say, "God, send Your angels to help me," and He will command His army to act.

Dear God, thank You for angels who watch
over me and keep me safe. Amen.

ARMOR OF GOD

*Put on the full armor of God, so that you can take
your stand against the devil's schemes.*

Ephesians 6:11 niv

In ancient days, soldiers wore armor made of metal. When they went into battle, the armor protected their bodies from weapons. What if there was a kind of armor you could put on to protect you from all the scary stuff that worries you? The Bible says there is! Jesus' follower Paul wrote that God gives us things to help us stand up to worries and trouble. God's armor is made up of truth, righteousness (being right with God), peace, faith, the Word of God (the Bible), and salvation. (*Salvation* means trusting in Jesus to save us from sin.) When worries and troubles come your way, you can use each part of God's armor to protect you.

---

*Dear God, thank You for giving me things I can use
against all my worries and fears. Thank You for
loving me and wanting to protect me. Amen.*

TAKE THAT, SATAN!

Jesus said to the devil, "Get away, Satan. It is written, 'You must worship the Lord your God. You must obey Him only.' "

MATTHEW 4:10

Satan spreads worry, doubt, and fear. When he tried to get Jesus to obey him, Jesus wouldn't have any part of it. "Get away, Satan!" Jesus said. Satan loves saying things that aren't true. He whispers inside your heart, "Nobody loves you," "You're ugly," "Everyone is better than you," "You're not smart enough." These are all lies! Get in the habit of using the truth part of God's armor to fight against those lies. When you hear Satan say bad things about you, send him away by responding with the truth. Tell Satan you are loved, smart, and just as good as everyone else. Tell him you are smart enough to accomplish whatever you set out to do. Then tell him you know it's the truth because God says so.

Dear God, You've given me the truth to use as a weapon against lies. Please help me use it wisely. Amen.

WEAR YOUR RIGHTEOUSNESS

Anyone can be made right with God by the free gift of His loving-favor. It is Jesus Christ Who bought them with His blood and made them free from their sins.

ROMANS 3:24

You've put on just one part of God's armor, the truth. Now it's time to add another. Put on your "righteousness" (that means being right with God). The righteousness part of your armor is created by believing in God's Son, Jesus, and wanting to become more like Him. You are made right with God by learning all you can about Jesus and trying your best to follow what He taught. With Jesus as your best friend, you can be sure He will always be on your side. Jesus will fight alongside you against any worries or trouble. The righteousness part of your armor is an important reminder that God's Son is all-powerful. You can trust in His power to help you knock down all your worries and fears.

Dear Jesus, thank You for fighting with me against whatever trouble comes my way. Amen.

PUT ON SOME PEACE

*"I have told you these things so you may have peace
in Me. In the world you will have much trouble.
But take hope! I have power over the world!"*

JOHN 16:33

Add some peace to your armor. Peace protects your heart from worry getting inside and staying there. The peace part of your armor will only work if you trust in Jesus. He never said you wouldn't have trouble. Jesus said the opposite: "In the world you will have much trouble." But then He said, "Take hope! I have power over the world!" When you trust in Jesus' power over the world, He fills your heart with His peace. Along with trusting Him, you can strengthen your peace by slowing down and being still. Instead of allowing unsettling thoughts to sink in, think about Jesus' power. Get busy helping others with their problems rather than worrying about your own. Do these things, and Jesus' peace will guard your heart.

---

*Dear Jesus, help me to trust in You even more than I do
right now. Please fill my heart with Your peace. Amen.*

ARE YOU READY?

*"Get the horses ready and get on them! Take your
places with your head-coverings on! Make your spears
shine, and put on your heavy battle-clothes!"*

JEREMIAH 46:4

Imagine yourself standing in front of a full-length mirror wearing
your armor. You're confident that you're ready to resist Satan and
any trouble he throws at you. You've armed yourself with truth,
righteousness, and peace. Truth protects you from Satan's lies.
That's important. Righteousness is being sure you can call on Jesus'
power in all circumstances. How could you go wrong with Him
leading you into battle? You've added peace, the part that guards
your heart from worries creeping in. That's all good, but it's still not
enough protection. When Paul wrote about God's armor, he said,
"Put on the *full* armor of God." The three most protective parts of
your armor are still missing. Can you guess what they are?

---

*Dear God, I have truth, righteousness, and peace.
Please provide me with the rest of my armor so it
will be super strong and complete. Amen.*

BE COURAGEOUS; BE STRONG!

Be on your guard; stand firm in the faith;
be courageous; be strong.

1 CORINTHIANS 16:13 NIV

Faith is the strongest part of your armor because faith gives you courage. Imagine going into battle without courage. Fear would make you turn and run away. Faith is believing in what you can't see. You won't *see* Satan whispering, "You're not good enough," but you know he's there because you hear his words inside your heart. You see the trouble he causes. The same is true about God. You can't see Him, but you hear His encouraging words inside your heart. You see the good things He does. You will tap into God's power when you trust He is real and has already defeated Satan. When you listen to God speaking His words inside your heart and trust He is real, you can courageously stand up to any trouble that gets in your way.

Dear God, strengthen my armor with faith. I believe
that You are real, You love me, and You will give
me courage to stand up to trouble. Amen.

MORE POWERFUL THAN A LASER SWORD

*God's Word is living and powerful. It is sharper
than a sword that cuts both ways.*

HEBREWS 4:12

In the world of movies and imagination, futuristic soldiers fight with laser swords. These make-believe light swords can cut, burn, and melt most substances. The only thing that can stop a laser sword is another laser sword. But that's in the movies! There's a real weapon that can destroy a futuristic soldier wielding a laser sword—or any other trouble that comes your way. That weapon is the Bible, God's Word. The Bible is filled with God's instructions and promises. When you read and remember what you've read, God's Word will be inside your heart. If you are in trouble, God's Word will encourage you, guide you, and make you strong. Add it as one of the most protective parts of your armor. Practice using it so you will be ready whenever you need it.

---

*Dear God, when I read my Bible, help me to understand
its words. Guide me to use them against any kind
of trouble that comes my way. Amen.*

SAVED FROM SIN

You will get what your faith is looking for, which
is to be saved from the punishment of sin.

1 PETER 1:9

Without Jesus, you can't fight a battle against Satan and win. God sent His Son, Jesus, to earth to save us from sin. (Sin means doing things that displease God.) Jesus was nailed to a cross to die, and all the world's sin—all the bad stuff people would ever do—was placed on Him. When Jesus died, your sins died along with Him. Being saved from sin is called "salvation." Salvation is the most powerful part of your armor, because salvation is knowing that you belong to Jesus and that He will be your protector. If you trust in Jesus to save you from your sin, He will send His Holy Spirit to come and live inside your heart. He will be with you forever as your protector and friend. Jesus defeated Satan when He gave His life on the cross and then rose from the dead three days later. As you trust Jesus, He will give you victory in every battle you face against Satan.

Dear Jesus, thank You for saving me from sin. You make
my armor complete, and I'm ready for battle. Amen.

GOD WILL FIGHT FOR ME

"The Lord says to you, 'Do not be afraid or troubled because of these many men. For the battle is not yours but God's.'"

2 CHRONICLES 20:15

Now you're wearing God's armor to protect you from all the bad stuff. When you remember that you have your armor on, you'll discover you don't worry as much. You have the super powerful extra layer of protection that comes from trusting Jesus. When you trust in the strength of your armor, you can stand up to trouble. When you put on the armor of God, all the scary stuff won't seem as scary anymore. Second Chronicles 20:15 says not to be afraid when you go into battle against trouble because the battle isn't yours—it's God's. God is the one with the power over all kinds of trouble, and He will fight for you.

---

*Dear God, whenever I face something scary,
I won't worry or be afraid because You will fight
for me. The battle is Yours, not mine. Amen.*

YOU KNOW THE DRILL

"Do not fear, for I am with you. Do not be afraid, for I am your God. I will give you strength, and for sure I will help you."

ISAIAH 41:10

Does your school have emergency drills? Some kids find them scary because the drills cause them to think about unpleasant things. If emergency drills make you jittery, you might feel better if you think of them as one more layer of protection added to your armor. In Isaiah 41:10, God says, "Do not fear, for I am with you. Do not be afraid, for I am your God." Then He makes this promise to you: "I will give you strength, and for sure I will help you." Emergency drills are another way God protects you. They help you get ready for trouble if it were to happen. The next time your school has a drill, instead of thinking about scary stuff, think about God keeping you safe. Imagine Him power-coating your armor, making it super strong.

Dear God, thank You for giving me a new way of thinking about emergency drills. Thank You for adding even more protection to my armor. Amen.

SAFE AT HOME

Good thinking will keep you safe.

PROVERBS 2:11

Your principal, teachers, and others in your community are always thinking about ways to keep you safe in school. It's up to you and your parents, though, to think of ways to keep you safe at home. The Bible says, "Good thinking will keep you safe." Good thinking is wise thinking. Talk with your parents about making your home safe by having things like smoke alarms, a carbon monoxide detector, a fire extinguisher, a first-aid kit. . . Can you think of a few more things you might need? Does your family have a plan in place if there's trouble? It's wise to have a family meeting to plan how you would handle an emergency. Making your house safe and having a plan for emergencies will help you worry less. It's always good to plan ahead and be prepared.

Dear God, thank You for reminding me of ways my family can feel safe at home. Please give my parents wise thinking to prepare our family for any kind of emergency. Amen.

MOVING DAY

"I will go before you and make the hard places smooth."

ISAIAH 45:2

What if your parent got a job in another state and your family had to move? The idea of living somewhere unfamiliar can be scary. Moving means packing up everything you own. As your family packs things in boxes, your home won't seem so comfortable and cozy anymore. You might feel lost in the middle of letting go of your old home and moving to a new one. The good news is this: God is where you're going! He's already at your new house or apartment, and He has made a plan for you and your family. It's a good plan. You might feel a little unsettled for a while, but as soon as you get to your new place, God will begin helping you make it a home. Before long, you will feel comfortable and cozy there.

Dear God, I'd rather not move. But if I have to go, I'm glad You've gone ahead of me to make my new home a place where I'll feel comfortable and safe. Amen.

CHANGE

"Do not remember the things that have happened
before. Do not think about the things of the past. See,
I will do a new thing. It will begin happening now."

ISAIAH 43:18–19

Life is filled with changes, especially when you're a kid. Some changes make you happy—for example, when your parents trust you with a new and more grown-up responsibility or when you finally go to a school where you have your own locker. Other changes are hard—adjusting to life if your parents get divorced, for instance, or starting a new school where you don't know anyone. You can trust God to help you through all the changes that happen in your life. When you face a difficult change, God says, "Do not think about the things of the past." Change will be easier when you keep moving forward. "See, I will do a good thing!" God says. His plan for you is always good.

Dear God, when a difficult change comes along,
clear my head of any scary thoughts. Help me to
trust in You and keep moving forward. Amen.

WRITE IT DOWN

*Then the Lord said to Moses, "Write this
in a book, to be remembered."*
EXODUS 17:14

God sometimes told men in the Bible to write things down. The men who wrote the Bible recorded God's words and also told about things that happened. Writing things down not only helps us remember, but it helps us not to be afraid. When we write about our problems or what scares us, we can look back and see how God worked everything out for our good. When you face a change, write the pros (what might be good about it) and cons (what might be not-so-good). Focus on the good stuff. If you have scary thoughts about something that might happen, write about that too. List reasons why you are afraid and reasons why you shouldn't be afraid. Don't forget to pray about your worries. God is waiting and ready to help.

---

*Dear God, thank You for giving me a new way to deal
with my worries. I will try writing about them, and I will
trust You to work everything out for good. Amen.*

TALK ABOUT IT

Hear my prayer, O God. Listen to the words of my mouth.

PSALM 54:2

Whether you're worried about a big change or anything else, don't keep your worries bottled up inside. Talk about them. Tell your parent or another trusted adult about what's bothering you. Talk about your feelings. Grown-ups have faced many troubles and changes in their lives, and they'll have good ideas to help with your worries. When you share your troubles, it helps you remember that you're not alone. Talking helps get rid of some of the scary feelings you've kept inside. Don't ever be afraid to talk with someone about your worries. Most of all, talk with God. Go someplace quiet and tell Him everything. He hears every word. God's love for you is bigger than all your troubles, and you can be sure He will comfort and help you.

Dear God, You are the best listener and helper. Thank You for being here for me. When I'm worried about something and even a little afraid, lead me to people who will listen and help. Amen.

BE HOPEFUL

*Be happy in your hope. Do not give up when trouble
comes. Do not let anything stop you from praying.*

ROMANS 12:12

If something is bothering you, which do you think would be best
to do: worry that things might get worse or be hopeful? One dark
night, Jesus' disciples (His followers) were in a boat on the water.
They had trouble rowing against a strong wind. Suddenly they saw a
figure walking toward them! The men were afraid until they heard
a voice saying, "Take hope. It is I. Do not be afraid!" It was Jesus
walking on the water. He came over to them, got in the boat, and
the wind stopped. Jesus has power over the world. He can walk on
water and do any other amazing thing you can imagine. The Bible
says Jesus is our hope. Whenever you face something scary, put
your hope in Jesus. Instead of worrying, be hopeful that things will
turn out all right.

---

*Dear Jesus, rather than worry, I will put my hope in
You. I will trust You to work everything out. Amen.*

HOME ALONE

God has said, "I will never leave you or let you be alone."
HEBREWS 13:5

Staying home alone is a very grown-up responsibility, and when your parents decide the time is right, they will trust you to be on your own. The first time you're alone in the house, along with feeling happy you might feel a little unsettled. You might even start worrying about some what-ifs. What if something happened and you needed Mom and Dad? What if they didn't answer if you called? It's important to remember that you are never alone. God promises never to leave you or let you be alone. Your parents wouldn't leave you home alone if they felt it was unsafe. You can be sure they will check in with you to see how things are going. Enjoy your new freedom, treat it responsibly, and trust that everything will be okay.

Dear God, being home alone is a privilege. I want to show my parents that I can be trusted. Lead me to do what's right and safe, and remind me that I'm never alone. You are always with me. Amen.

PRIVILEGES

*"He that is faithful with little things is faithful with big things also.
He that is not honest with little things is not honest with big things."*
LUKE 16:10

You're growing up, and you want to do more grown-up things. You're ready to make more decisions on your own and be more independent. You want to have more to say about what you wear, how you spend your money, and where you go and when. You want to stay up later, set your own schedule, and maybe be allowed more screen time. Those are all special privileges that require your parents to trust you. You will earn their trust by being responsible for the little things. If your parents see you following their rules and making wise decisions, they might allow you bigger privileges. The key to getting what you want is good behavior. Behave in ways that please your parents—and God.

---

*Dear God, I'm a responsible kid, and I want to earn
more grown-up privileges. Help me to behave in ways
that show my parents I'm trustworthy. Amen.*

PARENTS

*Children, as Christians, obey your parents. This is the
right thing to do. Respect your father and mother.*

EPHESIANS 6:1–2

Parents can be a challenge. You know it's true. When you want to do something and your parents say no, it's frustrating—irritating, even! You don't like all the control your parents have over you because you feel you're ready for more privileges and doing more things on your own. How do you handle difficult parents? You obey and respect them. That's what the Bible says to do, and it's the right thing to do. God gave Moses ten special rules for all people to follow. The Ten Commandments guide people to live in ways that please God. One of those commands is "Honor your father and mother." That means honoring them all the time, not just when you feel like it. By working hard at obeying and respecting your mom and dad, you will open the door to getting more of what you want.

---

*Dear God, even when they're being difficult,
help me to respect and honor my parents. Amen.*

TEN GREAT LAWS

Then Moses called all Israel, and said to them, "Listen,
O Israel, to the Laws which I speak in your hearing
today. Learn them and be careful to live by them."

DEUTERONOMY 5:1

The Ten Commandments God gave Moses are for all people, not just those who lived in Moses' time.

1. Put God before anyone or anything else.
2. Worship only Him.
3. Always use respect when saying God's name.
4. On Sunday, take time off to honor God.
5. Respect your parents.
6. Don't murder anyone.
7. Be faithful to the person you marry.
8. Don't steal.
9. Don't lie.
10. Don't be jealous of others.

God's Ten Commandments tell us to put God first and honor Him. They help us remember to treat others in ways pleasing to God. Memorize them and store them inside your heart. Do your best to follow them. God's special rules will help you not to be tricked by Satan to do things God won't like.

Dear God, I will do my best to follow Your laws. Amen.

IN FIRST PLACE—GOD!

"Have no gods other than Me."

EXODUS 20:3

God wants to be first in your life. He wants to be more important to you than anyone or anything else. Why? Because God deserves first place. He created the earth and everything in it. He rules the earth and its people, as well as the entire universe. Everything belongs to Him. God made you. You belong to God. He created you in love and gave you the privilege of living on His earth. If you make Him more important than anything else He will guide you through life, lead you to do great things, and give you strength to stand up to any trouble that gets in your way. Think about it. Is God more important to you than all the people in your life, than your pets, your favorite toys—your favorite anything? Learn to put God first by starting your day talking with Him in prayer. Then talk with Him all day and listen for His words inside your heart guiding you to do what's right.

Dear God, help me to put You first, ahead of everything else. Amen.

FALSE GODS

"Do not make a false god for yourselves, or anything
that is like what is in heaven above or on the earth
below or in the water under the earth."

DEUTERONOMY 5:8

What do you think a false god is? In Bible times, people often made statues and worshipped them as if they were real. But there are other kinds of false gods. Anyone or anything that you make more important than God is a false god. Imagine your most favorite person in the world. If you loved that person more than you love God, it would be as if you knelt in front of that person the way you would kneel before God. If you loved basketball or any other sport more than God, it would be like you kneeling courtside and worshipping the playing field. For everything to be okay in your life, it's important to make God your one-and-only God. Love Him more than anything else.

Dear God, You've helped me see that I have to get my priorities
straight. You are the only one worthy of worship and praise. Amen.

WORSHIP HIM

"All the earth will worship You and sing praises to
You. They will sing praises to Your name."

PSALM 66:4

When you feel worried, crabby, or sad, worshipping God will help. Worshipping Him means telling Him through words and actions that you think He's awesome. When you pray, you can worship God by telling Him you appreciate and love Him. You can worship Him by thanking Him. You could say, "Thank You, God, for getting me to the bus stop on time this morning." "Thank You, God, for this sunny day." "Thank You, God, for pancakes for breakfast." "Thank You, God, for my family and friends." There are endless things to thank Him for. You worship God by putting Him first and doing your best to please Him. You worship Him by singing the praise songs and hymns you learn at church. Worshipping God turns your thoughts toward Him instead of toward your troubles.

Dear God, I praise You! I think You're awesome, and I love You.
Thank You, God, for blessing me in so many wonderful ways. Amen.

GOD'S AMAZING LOVE

We have come to know and believe the
love God has for us. God is love.

1 JOHN 4:16

On days when your parents aren't cooperating, your siblings are driving you crazy, and no one seems to be on your side, you might think, *Nobody loves me.* That couldn't be further from the truth! It's a fact that a bunch of people love you. They might not be acting all lovey toward you right now, but underneath their bad moods they love you—a lot. When you're feeling unloved and alone, remember that God loves you. The Bible says, "God is love." He created you so He could love you forever. You are God's child, and His love for you is perfect. If you feel unloved, run to God. Be still and spend time with Him. Imagine Him giving you a hug and saying, "I'm here, little one, and I love you."

Dear God, no one seems to be on my side today, but I know You are.
Wrap Your arms around me and remind me that I'm loved. Amen.

GOD'S AMAZING NAME

"Do not use the name of the Lord your
God in a false way."
EXODUS 20:7

Imagine if you had a question about an assignment and you shouted to your teacher, "Hey, you! I need some help." Or what if you greeted your mom with, "Hi, Louise (or whatever her name is). How's it going?" You know to be respectful. Instead of saying, "Hey, you!" or deciding to call adults by their first names, you show them respect by saying, "Mr., Mrs. or Ms., Grandma, Grandpa, Mom, Dad, Uncle John, Aunt Mary," and so on. There is one whose name deserves even more respect. God's name is to be respected above all others. God says in the Ten Commandments, "Respect My name!" It's not okay to use His name as a swear word, in a joke, or in any other disrespectful way. Be sure that when you speak of God, it's always with honor, respect, and love.

Dear God, Your name is more important than any other name.
When I say Your name, I will say it with respect. Amen.

SUNDAY

"Remember the Day of Rest, to keep it holy. Six days you will do all your work. But the seventh day is a Day of Rest to the Lord your God."

EXODUS 20:8–10

In His Ten Commandments, God says to set aside Sunday as a day to honor Him and rest. God created everything in six days. On the seventh day, He rested. God wants us to follow His example. Maybe you spend Sundays doing homework, chores, or other kinds of work. If you were to follow God's law, you would do those things ahead of Sunday and make Sunday a day of rest. Many businesses are open on Sundays, and some people have to work on Sundays. But you can spend Sunday honoring God's law. You can attend church and also have extra worship time at home with your family. You can spend time resting together, playing games, reading. . . Can you think of other ways to rest and honor God?

Dear God, thank You for reminding me that Sunday is a special day to rest and honor You. Amen.

LAW NUMBER SIX—DO NOT KILL

"Do not kill other people."

EXODUS 20:13

It's important not only to know and remember God's Ten Commandments but also to think hard about what they mean. One of His laws says, "Do not kill." When you think about that law, does your mind travel to someone causing harm to another person's body? That's one way to think about it. But "Do not kill" could also mean something like "Don't kill a person's self-confidence." If you are mean to people or say things to put them down, you can hurt their feelings so deeply that you kill all the good feelings they have about themselves. Be careful not to hurt people. Don't hurt their bodies, and don't hurt their feelings. Do your very best to be careful with how people feel about themselves. Let them know they are good enough just as they are.

Dear God, You've given me a new way to think about Your law. I promise to try even harder not to hurt anyone's feelings. Amen.

BE FAITHFUL

"Be faithful in marriage."

Exodus 20:14 CEV

To be faithful to someone means keeping your promises, being trustworthy, and always being there to help and support the other person, no matter what. When a man and woman get married, God expects them to be faithful to Him and also to each other. "Be faithful in marriage" is another of His Ten Commandments. But faithfulness isn't just for married people. God expects us to be faithful to our friends, family members, and others. Think about it. Do you keep your promises? Can people trust you? If a friend needed you, would you stop whatever you were doing to help? If you answered yes, then you are a faithful friend. Faithful friends are the best kind of friends because they'll help you remember that everything will be okay. God is that kind of friend. He keeps His promises, is always trustworthy, and helps you—even *before* you need Him.

Dear God, thank You for always being faithful to me.
Please help me to be a faithful friend to others. Amen.

THAT'S MINE!

"Do not steal."

EXODUS 20:15

God's commandment "Do not steal" is another to think about and obey. You learned when you were younger that stealing things is wrong. But you might not know you can steal more than things. What if you were jealous of time your parent spent with your brother and you said, "That's mine! His time belongs to me!" Or what if you interrupted someone who was speaking and said, "My turn! Those words belong to me!" You can steal time meant for someone else. You can steal words someone wanted to say. If someone was proud of an accomplishment and you criticized their work, you could steal their pride. If someone had a goal in mind and you told them, "You'll never be able to do it," you could steal their dream. Think about what others need, and don't take what doesn't belong to you.

Dear God, I hadn't thought about stealing time from someone, or words or pride. Help me to think about what others need and only take what's mine. Amen.

JEALOUSY

If you have jealousy in your heart and fight to have many things, do not be proud of it.

JAMES 3:14

Another of God's Ten Commandments reminds us not to be jealous of what others have. You might not have the coolest clothes or the biggest house, the best grades in your class, or the height to sink a basket with every jump shot. If you want what someone else has, maybe you feel a little jealous. God wants us to be thankful for what we have. Thankfulness leads us closer to Him. When you get in the habit of thanking God for what you have, it takes your mind off what you don't have. Thankful people are happier people because even if they have just a little, they always find something to be grateful for. What are you thankful for today? See how many things you can add to your list.

Dear God, forgive me for wanting more than I have. I have so much to be grateful for. Thank You, God, for blessing me. Amen.

IT'S ALL ABOUT LOVE

I may be able to speak the languages of men and even of angels,
but if I do not have love, it will sound like noisy brass.

1 CORINTHIANS 13:1

Jesus' follower Paul said everything is meaningless without love. Paul compared a world without love to a noisy brass band. Imagine a band with each player playing a different tune. What a noisy mess that would be! Love is the secret to everything being okay. If we loved one another all the time the way Jesus loves us, the world would be a perfect place. But the world is a little messed up. God sees what's going on in our imperfect world, and He's working to make it better by guiding us to become more loving. God sees when people show love by being caring and kind, and that makes Him happy. He sees when people love one another by being generous, giving, encouraging, and helpful. Can you think of other ways to spread God's love around?

Dear God, teach me to love others the way You love them. Amen.

IT'S OKAY TO WALK AWAY

Love does not give up.

1 CORINTHIANS 13:4

If you treated someone with kindness and love and that person was always mean to you, your feelings would be hurt. If their meanness went beyond words, you might even feel a little afraid. When you've done your best to be good, kind, caring, forgiving, and still someone treats you badly, it's okay to walk away. No one wants you to get hurt. Walking away from bad behavior isn't the same as giving up on a person. Do you know you can still show love to those who hurt you? Praying for them is a loving thing to do. You can pray with the hope that God will help them turn their bad behavior around, and you can decide to forgive them even if they aren't sorry. It's okay to walk away from those who hurt you, but don't give up on loving them. Give them to God instead.

Dear God, I was being treated badly, so I walked away. Please teach loving-kindness to those who hurt me. Help me to forgive them even when they aren't sorry. Amen.

ROLE MODEL

Follow my example, as I follow the example of Christ.
1 CORINTHIANS 11:1 NIV

A role model is someone you admire, someone who behaves in ways you would like to behave. Maybe you have a role model. You might want to be more like your big sister or maybe like the boy in your class who is kind to everyone and has many friends. It's good to imitate the good examples set by others, but the best role model of all is Jesus. Read about Him in your Bible and think about how He behaved. Then follow His example. Notice how He handled people when they were difficult to get along with. Jesus always gave good advice and did the right thing. Sometimes Jesus walked away from people behaving badly; other times they walked away from Him. But Jesus kept on loving them and wanting them to do better. If you grow to be more like Jesus, you will become a good role model for others.

Dear Jesus, You are the best role model!
Lead me to become more like You. Amen.

UNSELFISH LOVE

Love does not put itself up as being important.

1 CORINTHIANS 13:4

Have you noticed that when people are in trouble, others hurry to help? After a hurricane, for example, people help one another clean up from the storm. If some are without power, others bring generators to help. Helpers come with food, water, clothing, and other supplies. Most of those helpers had things to do that day, but instead they gave their time to help others. Making someone else's needs more important than your own is another form of love. It's unselfish love. Can you think of a time someone loved you unselfishly? Maybe you were sick and your mom gave up what she wanted to do to stay home and care for you. Or maybe your dad went to your recital instead of staying home and watching a sports event on TV. When you love unselfishly, you help make the world a better place.

---

*Dear God, lead me to love unselfishly by putting
the needs of others ahead of my own. Amen.*

DO THE RIGHT THING

Love does not do the wrong thing.

1 CORINTHIANS 13:5

Imagine that your friend is about to break a rule. You know if someone finds out, he could be in a lot of trouble. You love your friend. You don't want him to be punished. What would you do? It wouldn't be right just to stand by, say nothing, and watch your friend do something you know is wrong. But if you told on him, that could get him in trouble too. Sometimes it's not easy to know what to do. If your friend was in danger of getting hurt or hurting someone, the right thing would be to tell somebody. Otherwise it would be good to encourage your friend not to break the rule. If he doesn't listen, it's not your fault. You aren't responsible for his behavior. Love always does what's right. If you're not sure what's right, think about how Jesus might handle the situation. Pray and ask Him for help.

---

*Dear Jesus, please guide me to do what's right,
especially when I can't decide. Amen.*

LET IT GO

Love does not get angry. Love does not remember the
suffering that comes from being hurt by someone.
1 CORINTHIANS 13:5

Your best friend started hanging out with other kids, and now you feel left out and left behind. Your feelings are hurt. You think, *I'm never going to forget how I feel right now.* You might even wish you could hurt your friend's feelings in return. It's okay to let your feelings out. But then let them go. When you hold on to anger and hurt, you only hurt yourself. Letting go of hurt feelings isn't an easy thing to do. But God will help you. This is a situation when talking with Him and praying for your friend is the right thing to do. In your heart, you still love your friend. That's why you hurt so much. Keep on loving your friend in your heart. Ask God to bring the two of you back together. Then trust Him to do what's right.

Dear God, please take away my hurt and anger.
Will You lead me back to my friend? Amen.

WHAT GOD WANTS

"My Father, if this must happen to Me, may
whatever You want be done."

MATTHEW 26:42

God wants you to ask Him for things, but God won't always give you what you ask for. That's because God knows best what you need. Maybe after your friend left you to hang out with someone else, you prayed, asking God to bring you and your friend back together. But that didn't happen; your friend moved on. God knows you deserve friends who love you and will stick by you no matter what. The person who used to be your friend and hurt your feelings might not be right for you anymore. Trust that God has some new friends waiting for you. All through your life, friends will come and go. Only a few will stay forever. Trust God with your requests. If He says no, believe it's because He wants you to have something even better.

Dear God, I wish You had said yes when I asked You to
lead me back to my friend. Help me understand that You
want something better for me. I trust You, God. Amen.

WHEN I DON'T UNDERSTAND

*Trust in the Lord with all your heart, and do not trust
in your own understanding. Agree with Him in all your
ways, and He will make your paths straight.*

PROVERBS 3:5–6

When you don't understand God's decisions, it's okay to tell Him so. Often it's hard to find good reasons for what God allows to happen. God's thoughts and His ways of doing things are so much greater than ours that it's impossible to understand Him. When you don't get what you want or when something unpleasant happens to you or someone you love, it's okay to say, "God, I don't understand." Ask Him to help you trust that His decision was right. The Bible says to agree with God that He does the right things. That's hard to do when you don't understand. But trust God anyway. When you can trust God without understanding Him, you'll get even closer to believing everything will be okay.

Dear God, I don't understand what You did, but I will trust You anyway. Your ways and thoughts are greater than mine. Amen.

STAND UP FOR WHAT'S RIGHT

Love is not happy with sin. Love is happy with the truth.

1 CORINTHIANS 13:6

What if you were at a friend's house and he put on a movie you knew you shouldn't watch? You have a choice to sit and watch the movie with him or to stand up for what you know is right. Standing up for what's right isn't always easy. God wants you to be courageous and say no. He understands that might be hard to do. So if you ask Him, God will give you the right words to say. God isn't happy when you allow sinful things into your eyes and ears. He is happy, though, when you speak up against those things. Tell your friend you'd rather watch a different movie or suggest the two of you do something else.

Dear God, when I stand up for what's right, I'm being a good role model for others, and I'm pleasing You too. Please give me courage to do what's right, especially when it's hard. Amen.

TRUE LOVE

Love believes all things. Love hopes for all
things. Love keeps on in all things.

1 CORINTHIANS 13:7

How would you describe true love? Maybe you said hugs and kisses, sweet words, love notes, snuggles. . . True love—Jesus' kind of love—is none of those things. Jesus' kind of love always looks for the good in people. His love is always hopeful. It believes people can and will do better. Jesus' kind of love keeps going even when people behave badly and do mean and hurtful things. Jesus loves even when He doesn't get love in return. He loves in ways that are caring, kind, and forgiving. His kind of love is what "true love" means. It's a perfect love. Practice showing others Jesus' kind of love. Look for the best in them, encourage and believe in them, and continue to love them even when they aren't acting lovable. Keep on loving them even when they don't love you back. If you love others like Jesus loves, your love for them will grow.

Dear Jesus, guide me to love others the way You love them. Amen.

FOREVER LOVE

Love never comes to an end.

1 CORINTHIANS 13:8

Have you heard someone say, "I love you to the moon and back"? The moon is 238,855 miles from Earth. A round trip would be 477,710 miles. That's far! But if you look at a map of the solar system, the moon appears close to Earth. And if you imagine beyond what you can see—the universe—the moon appears even closer. God's love is far greater than to the moon and back. His love extends beyond the universe all the way to forever. Forever has no beginning and no end. God loved you before you were born, He loves you now, and He will love you even after you die. He has a special place waiting for you in heaven where He will love you forever. When you trust in God's forever love, you'll know for sure that everything will be okay.

Dear God, Your love for me is greater than I can imagine. It stretches far beyond the moon and back, all the way from Earth to heaven. Amen.

THE BEST PROMISE EVER

*Jesus said to[Martha], ". . .Anyone who puts his trust
in Me will live again, even if he dies. Anyone who
lives and has put his trust in Me will never die."*

JOHN 11:25–26

When He lived on earth, Jesus made a promise to us. He said that everyone who trusts in Him will live again after they die. When Jesus died on the cross, His body was buried in a tomb. Three days later, He was alive again! Jesus did that to show us we can live again after we die. Jesus went up to heaven to be with God. That's what we will do too. Our bodies won't come to life on earth like Jesus' did, but if we put our trust in Him, our souls will go to heaven. In heaven we will have new and perfect bodies. Heaven is a perfect forever place where everything is always okay.

---

*Dear Jesus, I'm not afraid of going to heaven, because
You and others who love me are there. Amen.*

WHEN SOMEONE DIES

*"God will take away all their tears. There will be
no more death or sorrow or crying or pain."*

REVELATION 21:4

Maybe you know someone who died, or maybe you are afraid of losing someone close to you. When someone dies, people are sad. They feel sad because they will miss that person. God understands, and He promises to wipe away all their tears. It helps a little to remember that people who trust in Jesus never die. They leave their earthly bodies behind when they go to heaven, but they still are the same people in heaven as they were on earth—only better. In heaven they have perfect bodies that will never hurt or get sick. And because heaven is a perfect place, those who die never have bad feelings like sadness or anger. If you are feeling sad and missing someone who is in heaven, it's good to talk with someone about your feelings. If you are worried about someone dying, talk about that too.

---

*Dear God, if someone I love goes to heaven, I know I will feel
sad. But knowing they are with You brings me comfort. Amen.*

WE REMEMBER

These things I remember, and I pour out my soul within me.

PSALM 42:4

If you've been to a memorial service, you saw photos of the person who died and objects they owned that bring happy memories. At a roadside, you might see a small cross and other remembrance objects marking where someone lost their life in an accident. When someone dies, photos and objects that bring happy memories help ease the sadness. Maybe you went with your parents to a cemetery to plant flowers on a loved one's grave. You might have attended a Memorial Day event to remember soldiers who died serving their country. When someone dies, we remember how they were when they were alive and happy. Sharing good memories is one way people grieve. The memories and good feelings we have of those who die live on in our hearts. It's important to remember that Jesus made it possible for us to be together again with our loved ones in heaven. We are apart from them for a while, but we will see them again someday.

Dear God, please bring comfort to the families
and friends of those who have died. Amen.

WHEN A PET DIES

*"Are not two small birds sold for a very small piece
of money? And yet not one of the birds falls to the
earth without your Father knowing it."*

MATTHEW 10:29

We love our pets. They're our playmates and friends. Pets are family members, and when one dies, we are very sad. If you lose a pet, there's an empty place in your heart. That's because you loved your little friend. It might help to remember that no animal dies without God knowing it. God made all the animals. He cares for them, and we can imagine that when our pets die, God has a place for them in heaven. Some people imagine their pets crossing a rainbow bridge into heaven. If your pet dies, hold on to happy memories. You might even make a little memorial for your pet with a photo and remembrance objects. Trust God to comfort you. He knows your heart hurts, and He will help you.

---

*Dear God, my pet passed away, and I'm very sad. I imagine
my pet is with You now. Take good care of my pet, and
please help my heart not to hurt so much. Amen.*

WHAT IS A SOUL?

The Holy Writings say, "The first man, Adam, became a living soul."
1 CORINTHIANS 15:45

Your soul is a part of you that can't be seen. It holds all your thoughts, feelings, and emotions. God gave you a human body so you can walk, talk, see, hear, and more. But you are much more than your body. When God made your soul, He gave you your own special thoughts, feelings, and emotions. When your body dies, your soul—the part that makes you uniquely you—will still be alive. You will instantly have a new body in heaven, a perfect body. In heaven you will still be yourself. You will have your personality and all the good thoughts, memories, and feelings that were inside your heart. No one knows exactly what heaven is like, but it's God's home, so it must be amazing!

Dear God, thank You for giving me a soul. Please fill it up with what's good and pleasing to You. Amen.

WHAT IS HEAVEN LIKE?

"There are many rooms in My Father's house. If it were not so, I would have told you. I am going away to make a place for you. After I go and make a place for you, I will come back and take you with Me. Then you may be where I am."

JOHN 14:2–3

Jesus said that He is already making a place for you in heaven. Can you imagine what it might look like? Heaven is where Jesus and God live. Everyone in heaven worships and praises them. Heaven is a place filled with peace and joy. We imagine animals there because the Bible says that one day Jesus will come back to the earth riding through the sky on a white horse. A beautiful and pure white light shines throughout heaven. Heaven's gates are giant pearls, and its streets are made of gold. We can't imagine how totally beautiful heaven is, because there are things there that don't exist on earth. Someday when you get there, you will find many wonderful things to explore.

Dear God, thank You for saving a place for me in heaven. Amen.

SCARY THINGS

"When you pass through the waters, I will be with you. When you pass through the rivers, they will not flow over you. When you walk through the fire, you will not be burned."

ISAIAH 43:2

There's nothing wrong with feeling afraid. Every human who has ever lived has been afraid of something. People fear different things. Some love high places; others tremble when up high looking at the earth below. Some love to swim; others are afraid of water. What frightens people can change over time. For example, when you were little, you might have held on to your parent's hand because you were afraid of getting lost. Now that you're older, you want more independence and you'd be embarrassed to go everywhere holding Mom's hand. What are you afraid of today? Talking with someone about your fear is one way to let go of scary feelings. Talking with God is good too. He promises that whatever you are afraid of, He will be with you, helping you to be okay.

Dear God, when I am afraid, I will turn to You. Amen.

GIVE IT SOME THOUGHT

*The way of a fool is right in his own eyes, but
a wise man listens to good teaching.*

PROVERBS 12:15

Your little brother runs into your room in the middle of the night, climbs into bed with you, and pulls the covers over his head. "What's the matter?" you ask. He wails, "There's a monster under my bed!" You know that monsters don't exist, but he doesn't. You have to take him by the hand and show him there's nothing but a baseball glove and a candy bar hiding under his bed. Things become less scary when you have all the facts. You might not be scared of monsters anymore, but you're afraid of other things. Measure your fear against the truth. For example, you might be afraid a storm will destroy your house. Do the research, and you'll find it's more likely it won't happen than it will. Knowing the facts and listening to wise advice goes a long way in getting rid of your fears.

---

*Dear God, I worry about a lot of things that probably
won't happen. Please lead me to the truth. Amen.*

GIVE IT A TRY

"Rise up; this matter is in your hands. We will
support you, so take courage and do it."

Ezra 10:4 niv

Some of those things you're afraid of might not seem so scary if you give them a try. Maybe you want to play on the softball team but you're afraid you won't be good enough. The more you think about it, the more what-ifs enter your mind. "What if I miss hitting the ball and people laugh at me?" "What if I strike out and that makes my team lose the game?" "What if I fall and get hurt?" All those what-ifs could stop you from even trying to play. You could miss out on having a great time and making new friends. Remember, there are people who care about you who will help and support you when you tackle something new. So what are you waiting for? Give it a try.

Dear God, I would like to try _____, but I'm afraid.
Please give me courage to try. Send people who
will encourage and support me. Amen.

PLAY THE WHAT-IF GAME

"Come now, let us think about this together," says the Lord.

ISAIAH 1:18

There's a little mind game you can play when something worries you. Start with a what-if. Then think it through in a positive way. Here's an example:

- *What if I were hurt in an accident:*
- People would come immediately to help me.
- EMTs would take me to the hospital.
- Doctors and nurses would take good care of me.
- They would fix what's wrong with me.
- I would get better and go home.
- Everything would be okay.

Sometimes thinking through a what-if will help it seem not so scary. Even if your what-if was "What if I die?" you could remember that if that were to happen, you would be in heaven with God and others who love you. The likelihood of you dying anytime soon isn't very great, so don't worry. Do your best to be happy and enjoy every day.

---

*Dear God, sometimes the what-ifs make me feel
afraid. Remind me that whatever happens, You
are in charge, and it will be okay. Amen.*

ONE *SSSSSTEP* AT A TIME!

The steps of a good man are led by the Lord.

PSALM 37:23

If you were afraid of snakes, the sight of one could send you running. What if your cousin had a pet snake? Being afraid of his snake might keep you from visiting his house; or if you did visit, you might worry that the snake was out of its tank or cage. You could keep on being afraid, or you could tackle your fear one step at a time. First, you could get used to looking at the snake inside its enclosure from a distance. Then you could watch your cousin interact with it outside the cage. Little by little you could move closer to the snake. With each step, you might be less afraid. Your goal is to touch it—maybe even to like touching it and make friends with it. Fear of something can go away if you work at it one step at a time. Trust God to help you.

Dear God, let's tackle my fear together, one step at a time. Amen.

GROWN-UP STUFF

Do not worry yourself because of those who do wrong.

PROVERBS 24:19

Are you worried about something going on with the grown-ups in your life? Maybe your parents aren't getting along, an older sibling is in trouble, your mom lost her job, your dad moved out. . . Kids worry about all kinds of grown-up things. But when parents don't get along or are out of work, or someone gets into trouble or behaves badly, it's not your fault. You didn't cause it to happen, and you can't fix it. Big problems like those are for grown-ups to handle. When you face big stuff, give your worries to God. Hold even tighter to Him and soak up all the love He has for you. Hang out with kids who know and love God. Form a prayer group with them and pray for one another concerning the problems you face. Remember, no problem is too big for God. You can trust Him with all your worries.

Dear God, I'm worried about stuff going on at home. Please help me remember that it's not my fault. I'm trusting You to help. Amen.

WHEN A PARENT CRIES

He gives us comfort in all our troubles. Then we can
comfort other people who have the same troubles.
We give the same kind of comfort God gives us.
2 CORINTHIANS 1:4

It can be worrisome to see a parent or another grown-up cry. You expect adults to be strong all the time and to face every problem like a superhero. Grown-ups do their best to be strong for their kids in all circumstances, but sometimes they grieve. Their feelings spill out, just like yours do. When you see a grown-up cry, your first thought might be to walk away and give them privacy. That would be okay. But think about what makes you feel better when you cry and are sad. Grown-ups need hugs, someone to hold their hand, and kind and caring words, just like you do. When a grown-up cries, it helps them get their feelings out so they can restore their strength and go on. Have you seen your parent cry? What did you do?

Dear God, everyone cries sometimes. When grown-ups I
love are sad, show me how to comfort them. Amen.

OVERWHELMED

"Come to Me, all of you who work and have
heavy loads. I will give you rest."

MATTHEW 11:28

"Overwhelmed" is when you feel everything is too much to handle on your own. It's when all your worries—school worries, friend worries, current event worries, grown-up worries—pile up until the pile is so big you can't see beyond it. Everyone feels overwhelmed sometimes. This feeling can disguise itself as crabbiness, sadness, or even anger. If you feel overwhelmed, it's best to just stop. Stop for a little while, rest, and remember that everything will be okay. Shift your thoughts to worshipping and praising God. Try this: Write down each worry, one by one. For each, write down why you know that God is handling it. You might write things like: "God is bigger than my worries." "There is nothing God can't handle." "God loves me." What else? . . .

Dear God, so much is going on lately, and I'm worried
about many things. Help me remember that You are in
control and that everything will be all right. Amen.

THE GOOD THING

"Only a few things are important, even just
one. Mary has chosen the good thing."
LUKE 10:42

The Bible tells about two sisters, Mary and Martha, who were Jesus' good friends. When He came to their town, Jesus sometimes stayed with them. One day when Jesus was there, Martha was busy preparing supper. She worked hard while Mary sat on the floor near Jesus, listening to Him teach. This irritated Martha. She went to Jesus and said, "Do You see that my sister is not helping me? Tell her to help me." Jesus said to her, "Martha, Martha, you are worried and troubled about many things. Only a few things are important, even just one. Mary has chosen the good thing. It will not be taken away from her" (Luke 10:40–42). What do you think "the good thing" was? Mary had chosen Jesus. She made Him more important than anything she worried about, even the work that had to get done.

Dear Jesus, it is good to make You more important than anything else. When I put You first, everything else falls into place. Amen.

WHEELCHAIRS, CRUTCHES, AND SCARS

God does not show favor to one man more than to another.

ROMANS 2:11

What if you hurt both your legs and you had to be in a wheelchair for a while? When you went to school, how would you feel if you were treated differently by your friends? Whether kids are in wheelchairs, walking with crutches, or otherwise have trouble getting around, they want to be treated the same as their peers. Kids who have scars, pimples, or other marks on their bodies don't want to be treated differently either. What would you do if you heard or saw someone make fun of a friend in a wheelchair or someone with a scar on her face? What are some ways you can include *all* kids so no one feels left out?

Dear God, it doesn't matter what we look like on the outside because in our hearts we're all just kids. I don't want anyone to be left out or treated differently. Amen.

HIDDEN DISABILITIES

Care about them as much as you care about yourselves
and think the same way that Christ Jesus thought.
PHILIPPIANS 2:4–5 CEV

Many differences can't be seen. Maybe you know someone at school who can't see or hear well, or a kid who uses an inhaler for breathing problems caused by asthma. Some kids have allergies to certain foods. Maybe you know someone who has trouble speaking and their words sound different or strange. You might have friends with learning differences; it isn't that they're not smart, but their brains just work differently. Being too worried or afraid can be an issue that affects how kids behave. Bad headaches and stomachaches can be issues too. If you know someone with a hidden difference that causes hardship, keep your eyes open for ways you can help. The Bible says to think the way Jesus thought and care about others as much as you care about yourself.

Dear God, please help me to be sensitive and recognize hidden differences and hardships. Show me how to include kids who have special needs, and teach me to be helpful. Amen.

TUNE IN

Someone's thoughts may be as deep as the ocean,
but if you are smart, you will discover them.

PROVERBS 20:5 CEV

Empathy is a word that means "tuning in to how others feel." It's being able to put yourself in someone else's shoes and understand their feelings. For example, if your sister is sad because she didn't get invited to a party, you understand what sadness feels like. If your brother is angry because someone cheated to win a game, you understand what anger feels like. If your friend is afraid of spiders, you understand what fear feels like. The reasons for someone feeling sad, angry, or afraid might be different, but you can understand those feelings because you've felt them yourself. When you are sensitive to how someone is feeling, you can be understanding and helpful. You can treat the other person the way you would want to be treated.

Dear God, lead me to be aware and sensitive to how
others are feeling. Help me to be more tuned in. Amen.

I HEAR YOU

If one gives an answer before he hears,
it makes him foolish and ashamed.

PROVERBS 18:13

If you understood that your brother felt angry because someone cheated, would it be best to say, "I get it! That happened to me," and tell him all about your experience? Or would it be better to ask, "What happened?" and then listen to his story? Your own experience gives you empathy for your brother's feelings—you know you would feel angry and upset if someone cheated. But instead of talking about yourself, it would be better to make the conversation all about your brother. You could ask him questions like, "How did that make you feel?" "Are you feeling less angry now?" You should tune out everything else and listen carefully to his words. A good listener listens quietly and carefully. After you heard his story, you could say, "I understand. Is there anything I can do to help?" Being a good listener is a great way to show others you care.

Dear God, teach me to become a better listener. Amen.

BOUNDARIES

Don't move a boundary marker set up by your ancestors.
PROVERBS 22:28 CEV

You might not be sure how someone is feeling. If your mom is unusually quiet, you'll think something is going on. Is she sad? Worried? Angry? Maybe she's just concentrating on what she's doing or thinking about something she needs to do. If you aren't sure about how someone feels, it's okay to ask. You could say something like, "I notice you're quiet. Are you okay?" or "You're a little quieter than normal. Is something bothering you?" Then tune in and listen. Your mom might tell you how she's feeling, or she might not. Most people have boundaries—things they don't feel comfortable talking about. If someone isn't willing to share their feelings, it's best to be understanding and give them space. You can help by being considerate and kind, and by praying.

Dear God, when something is bothering my mom or someone else and I'm not sure what it is, help me to be thoughtful and give them space. And please help them to be okay. Amen.

MORE BOUNDARIES

"But whoever is the reason for one of these little children who believe in Me to fall into sin, it would be better for him to have a large rock put around his neck and to be thrown into the sea."

MATTHEW 18:6

Boundaries are all about saying no. Everyone has boundaries, imaginary lines they don't want others to cross. Some boundaries are physical. For example, you've learned about good touches and bad touches. You know what's comfortable and right, and you know what's not. If someone were to try to cross that physical boundary, you should say no and also tell a trusted adult. Other boundaries have to do with your own behavior. You've set a boundary between right and wrong behavior. If someone were to lead you toward doing what's wrong to get you to cross that boundary, you shouldn't allow it. *No* is a very powerful word, and you should use it whenever you feel something is uncomfortable or wrong.

---

*Dear God, if someone tries to cross my boundaries,
give me courage to tell them "No!" Amen.*

WHEN NOT TO COMPROMISE

They do not compromise with evil, and they walk only in his paths.
PSALM 119:3 NLT

When you hear the word *compromise*, you think of it as a good thing. *Compromise* means reaching an agreement with someone so you each get a little of what you want. For example, you want to watch a movie, but your sister wants to watch a different one. You compromise and watch something you'll both like. That's a good compromise. But there's a time you should never compromise. If someone wants you to do what's wrong, you shouldn't give in, not even a little. The Bible warns, "Do not compromise with evil." Anything God doesn't approve of is evil. If you compromise and do what's wrong, it gets easier to do it again. Satan is sneaky that way. He pulls you away from God and toward him a little at a time. So be careful that you compromise only when it leads to something good.

---

*Dear God, thank You for reminding me not to give in
to anything that leads me away from You. Amen.*

EMPATHY'S COUSIN— COMPASSION

Last of all, you must share the same thoughts and the same feelings. Love each other with a kind heart and with a mind that has no pride.

1 PETER 3:8

Empathy has a close relative called Compassion. They go hand in hand. It's awesome to tune in to how others feel and share their thoughts and feelings. But compassion goes beyond empathy. It is showing through your actions that you understand and care. You can show compassion by forgiving others for their mistakes, recognizing that everyone messes up sometimes. You can stand up for someone who is treated badly, lend a helping hand to those who are busy, and give to those in need. Compassion is hugging someone who feels sad, encouraging others to try, and being a friend to someone who is lonely. There are many compassionate acts of kindness. Can you think of several more? Think about compassion today. Be caring and kind to everyone you meet.

Dear God, show me how to add compassion to my empathy. Teach me to show others through my actions that I care. Amen.

CARING TOO MUCH

If one part of the body suffers, all the other parts suffer with it.

1 CORINTHIANS 12:26

Empathy and compassion are wonderful qualities to have. But did you know you can care too much? Caring too much is when you make other people's feelings your own. It's when you absorb their emotions like a sponge. If you add someone's problems to your own, you'll end up feeling worried, sad, and depressed. It's important to sort out which feelings belong to you and which belong to someone else. For example, if your mom is sad, it wouldn't help for you to feel sad too—two sad people aren't better than one. Instead, you could recognize that your mom is sad, show her compassion, and realize that's all you can do. If you feel yourself caring too much, it's okay to get your mind off the way others feel and do something fun. It doesn't mean you don't care.

Dear God, remind me that I'm a kid and it's not my job to fix what's going on with others. Their problems belong to them and to You, and I know You will work everything out. Amen.

TOO FAST, TOO SLOW

You who are young, be happy while you are young, and
let your heart give you joy in the days of your youth.
ECCLESIASTES 11:9 NIV

You hear about and see all kinds of worldly problems that are outside your control. Add to that problems at home and in your family that you can't do much about. If you're soaking up grown-up worries and problems, you might feel like you're growing up too fast. On the other hand, there are times when it feels like you're growing up too slow. There are tons of things you'd like to do, but you aren't yet old enough. You want responsibilities you believe you're ready for, but adults say no. Growing up too fast, not growing up fast enough—it can be overwhelming! Your job right now is to be happy and have fun. The Bible says so: "Be happy while you are young." Find joy in every day. You'll have plenty of time to worry about grown-up problems later on when you're a grown-up.

Dear God, help me to be happy and joyful every day. Amen.

I CAN'T SLEEP!

I will lie down and sleep in peace. O Lord, You alone keep me safe.

PSALM 4:8

When you lie down to sleep at night, worries can keep you awake. When your room is dark and quiet, the thoughts inside your head seem louder. When you have uninterrupted time to lie there and listen to yourself think, your busy mind can rob you of much-needed rest. You don't have to spend your night worrying, because God never sleeps. While you are sleeping, God is wide awake working out all your situations for good. Instead of thinking of your troubles when you can't sleep, think about Him. Trust that God is right there in your room with you. Psalm 4:8 says that while you are sleeping, God promises to keep you safe. When you lie down to sleep tonight, give Him all your worries. Then close your eyes, snuggle warm under the covers, and sleep in peace.

Dear God, when worries keep me awake at night, I will give them to You and sleep in peace. I know You are awake, and I trust You to watch over me. Amen.

COUNT THE STARS

He knows the number of the stars. He gives names to all of them.

PSALM 147:4

If you can't sleep, it helps to look at the stars. How many do you think there are? It's impossible to know for sure. Scientists estimate there are around two hundred billion trillion stars in the universe. That's a lot of stars! We don't know exactly how many, because the universe extends beyond what we can see or imagine. The Bible says God knows the number of stars, and He has named each one. God doesn't need to estimate how many stars there are. He knows exactly how many because He made them all. When you can't sleep, look at the stars and think about how great God is. That same God who hung each star is watching over you tonight. He knows exactly who you are, where you are, and what you are thinking, and He knows too that you need your rest. So say, "Good night." Have sweet dreams. God is in control, and everything is going to be all right.

Dear God, it's time for me to say good night.
We'll talk again in the morning. Amen.

GOD KNOWS

*"The Powerful One, the Lord, the Powerful
One, God, the Lord! He knows!"*

JOSHUA 22:22

God knows everything about the future. The Bible says, "There will come times of much trouble. People will love themselves and money. They will have pride and tell of all the things they have done. They will speak against God. Children and young people will not obey their parents. People will not be thankful, and they will not be holy. They will not love each other. No one can get along with them. They will tell lies about others. They will not be able to keep from doing things they know they should not do. They will be wild and want to beat and hurt those who are good. They will not stay true to their friends. They will act without thinking. They will think too much of themselves. They will love fun instead of loving God" (2 Timothy 3:1–4). That sounds like today's world, doesn't it? Don't let today's troubles worry you. God knows. He loves you, and He's watching over you all the time.

---

*Dear God, You are bigger than anything
that's worrying me today. Amen.*

ALL KINDS OF FAMILIES

See, how good and how pleasing it is for
brothers to live together as one!

PSALM 133:1

Families come in many different combinations. Some families have a mom, dad, and kids all living together in the same house. Others have just a mom and kids living together or a dad and kids. Sometimes kids live with their grandparents. Even just a husband and wife with no children can be a family. And some families are made up of people who aren't related but live together and care for one another. How would you describe your family? The Bible says it is good and pleasing when people live together as one. When family members are tuned in to one another and are caring and compassionate, they help one another to be okay. It's wonderful when all family members know and love God. Then they can share in His love and worship and praise Him together.

Dear God, thank You for my family. I want all
of us to know and love You. Amen.

FAMILY FUN

Be full of joy all the time.
1 THESSALONIANS 5:16

It's good when all members of a family spend time together. Here are some ideas you can suggest to your parents that will create happy and joyful vibes in your house and encourage togetherness: Have at least one mealtime together each day when you check in with one another to be sure everyone is doing okay. Turn off the phones and other electronics while you eat. Read a book aloud together a chapter a day, or make videos of your family singing and dancing together and then share them with Grandma and Grandpa or others. Plan one day each month when your family goes someplace to have fun—a day at the beach, a park, the zoo. . .A "together day" gives all family members something to look forward to. End each day by saying a prayer together before you go to bed. Spending time together makes a family stronger and happier. It helps each member be more tuned in to the others.

Dear God, bring my family together each
day for fellowship and fun. Amen.

FELLOWSHIP

*From now on you are not strangers and people who
are not citizens. You are citizens together with those
who belong to God. You belong in God's family.*

EPHESIANS 2:19

Maybe you've heard your pastor use the word *fellowship*. Fellowship is when people get together to share a group activity or just spend time together being friendly and having fun. Fellowship time at church might mean a potluck supper, a church picnic or festival, a holiday event, a concert, or even a church movie night. Being together with friends at church often feels like being part of a family, and it should! Everyone who believes in God and Jesus, His Son, is a member of God's family. God wants His family members to spend time together in fellowship. He wants them to encourage one another, build one another up, and love and care for one another. Do you have a church family?

---

*Dear God, I'm glad I'm a member of Your family.
Please lead me into fellowship with other
Christians who know and love You. Amen.*

UNEXPECTED CHANGES

You do not know about tomorrow. What is your life?
It is like fog. You see it and soon it is gone.

JAMES 4:14

An unexpected change can affect everyone in a family. Maybe you or someone you know has faced an unexpected change. Parents get divorced, a parent's job change or financial situation means the family has to move, an illness in the family shifts all the attention to the person who is sick, a single parent remarries and suddenly everyone has to adjust to new family members—there are many kinds of unexpected changes. The Bible says we can't be sure what will happen tomorrow. What we can be sure of, though, is God knows. Even when the future looks foggy and we don't know what's up ahead, God knows. If you are hit with an unexpected and unhappy or unsettling change, God is already helping you find your way through it. Trust Him to lead you to brighter days ahead.

Dear God, I didn't see that change coming. I'm holding on
tight to You, and I trust that You will help me. Amen.

ALL TOGETHER NOW

"A family cannot last if it is divided against itself."

MARK 3:25

Sometimes a mom or dad gets remarried, and that changes who lives together. There might be a stepmom or a stepdad and new sisters and brothers moving in or a new house to live in. Adjusting to new people and a new place can be challenging for everybody. It requires a lot of patience. If you were in that situation, what could you do to help everyone get along? You might decide to take things slow and remember that everyone is in the same situation. All family members are adjusting to being part of a blended family. You could give everyone space and put your tuning-in and compassion skills to use. Be a good listener and try to put yourself in the other person's shoes. Remember too that God is your heavenly Father, and nothing about Him has changed. He stays the same forever.

Dear God, it feels like everything is different except You. I'm grateful that You are the same God all the time and that I can count on You. Amen.

I WILL ALWAYS LOVE YOU

May you have much of God's loving-kindness and peace and love.

JUDE 1:2

When parents get divorced or when a new stepmom or stepdad becomes part of your family, always remember that your parents still love you. Your mom and dad might not live together in the same house anymore, but that hasn't changed how much they care for and love you. Your mom and dad will always love you. A stepmom or stepdad isn't a replacement mom or dad, but many times they will become family members whom you grow to trust and love. Let your mom and dad know that you need some time alone with them as you adjust to your changing family. Tell them how you feel, and especially let them know if you're worried about something or afraid. Focus on those things that haven't changed instead of what's different.

Dear God, I feel kind of lost right now. My family is changing. I know Mom and Dad love me. Help me to think about that and everything that hasn't changed. Amen.

MY OWN SPACE

My soul is quiet and waits for God alone.

PSALM 62:5

Everyone needs a place where they can be quiet and alone for a while. Do you have your own space, somewhere you can go to be quiet and rest with God? If you don't have a quiet space, ask Mom or Dad to help you make one. Create a place in the house or yard that's yours alone. It can be your special place to go when you want to spend time talking with God or resting in His presence. Ask others to be respectful of your space because you need to be alone there with God. Can you think of a spot in your house that might work? If there isn't enough room at home for everyone who wants a quiet spot, maybe you could have a place set aside where all family members can go when they need to be alone with God.

---

*Dear God, please help me find the perfect spot where
I can rest and be alone with You. Amen.*

MORNING PRAYERS

In the morning before the sun was up, Jesus went to a
place where He could be alone. He prayed there.

MARK 1:35

Jesus always had people around Him. Some were His helpers; others followed wherever He went so they could hear Him teach. Sometimes Jesus wanted to be away from everyone for a while so He could be alone with God. Mark 1:35 tells of a time when before sunrise Jesus went to a quiet place where He could be alone and pray. Jesus always made time to talk with His Father. Do you spend quiet time each morning talking with God? It's good to spend a few minutes talking with Him before starting your day. In the morning, you can tell God your plans and ask Him to guide you. Give it a try. Tomorrow morning, spend a few minutes praying before you go to school.

Dear God, good morning! I'm ready to start
my day. Please watch over and guide me today.
Help me to do what's right and good. Amen.

A DO-OVER DAY

This is the day that the Lord has made.
Let us be full of joy and be glad in it.

PSALM 118:24

Did you know that God allows do-overs? If you mess up and tell God you're sorry, He is quick to forgive and give you a do-over. And bonus—you get more than one! Even if you mess up a hundred million times, if you ask God for forgiveness, He will say, "I forgive you. Today you can try again." Isn't that wonderful? Every new day is a do-over. Think about that when you say your morning prayers. Tell God, "I'm sorry I messed up yesterday. I will do my best to try harder today." God doesn't want you dragging yesterday's mistakes into today. Instead, He says, "This is a brand-new day I've made. Be full of joy and glad in it." Begin every day knowing you are forgiven and loved. Then be joyful and glad.

Dear God, I messed up yesterday, and I'm sorry.
Thank You for giving me a do-over day. Amen.

GOD BLESS YOU

*"May the Lord bring good to you and keep you. May the
Lord make His face shine upon you, and be kind to you.
May the Lord show favor toward you, and give you peace."*

NUMBERS 6:24–26

"God bless you" is something people say when they hear a sneeze.
No one seems to know why we ask God to bless a sneezer. It's an
ancient custom. But whatever the reason for blessing someone,
a blessing is a good thing. Blessings are gifts from God. Numbers
6:24–26 in the Bible is an example of a blessing. God said to Moses,
"This is the way you should bring good to the people of Israel. Say to
them, 'May the Lord bring good to you and keep you. May the Lord
make His face shine upon you, and be kind to you. May the Lord
show favor toward you, and give you peace.'" Things like goodness,
safe-keeping, kindness, and peace are blessings—gifts from God.
Saying "God bless you" is you asking God to give someone His goodness. Who would you like to bless today?

---

*Dear God, please bless my family and friends
with all kinds of goodness. Amen.*

COUNT YOUR BLESSINGS

Surely you have granted him unending blessings and
made him glad with the joy of your presence.

PSALM 21:6 NIV

Blessings are God's gifts to us. Some blessings are big things like receiving an honor or award, being healed of an illness, winning a prize, getting a new baby sister or brother. . . Can you think of several other big blessings? Many blessings, though, are things we take for granted: the laughs we share with friends, sunny days, music, art, the clothes we wear, hot water, a roof over our heads. . .The greatest blessing of all is God giving us so much of Himself—His love, time, forgiveness, power, and strength, and most of all the blessing of His Son, Jesus. When your mind is filled with worry or trouble, it will help to count your blessings. Write them down and keep your eyes open for new blessings every day.

Dear God, thank You for Your blessings. You've given
me so many that I can't count them all. Amen.

THE GOOD SHEPHERD

"I am the Good Shepherd. The Good Shepherd
gives His life for the sheep."
JOHN 10:11

Long ago, shepherds stayed with their sheep day and night, watching over them, keeping them safe. Jesus said that He is our Shepherd. He is the Good Shepherd who watches over us all the time. Jesus never leaves us, not even for a minute. He says, "My sheep hear My voice and I know them. They follow Me" (John 10:27). If we wandered away and got lost, Jesus would come and find us. His love for us is so great that He gave His life so we can have forever life with Him in heaven. If ever you believe you are in danger, call out for Jesus. He knows where you are. He is always with you, so you never have to feel you are alone. In any kind of trouble, you can count on Jesus to keep you peaceful and calm.

Dear Jesus, You are always with me, watching
over me and keeping me safe. Amen.

PSALM TWENTY-THREE

The Lord is my Shepherd. I will have everything I need.

PSALM 23:1

Psalm 23 is one you should memorize to remind yourself that Jesus is with you:

"The Lord is my Shepherd. I will have everything I need. He lets me rest in fields of green grass. He leads me beside the quiet waters. He makes me strong again. He leads me in the way of living right with Himself which brings honor to His name. Yes, even if I walk through the valley of the shadow of death, I will not be afraid of anything, because You are with me. You have a walking stick with which to guide and one with which to help. These comfort me. You are making a table of food ready for me in front of those who hate me. You have poured oil on my head. I have everything I need. For sure, You will give me goodness and loving-kindness all the days of my life. Then I will live with You in Your house forever."

Dear Jesus, help me to memorize Your words
and keep them inside my heart. Amen.

I WILL PRAY FOR YOU

I always give thanks for you and pray for you.
EPHESIANS 1:16

When you pray, what do you pray for? It's good to ask God for what you want and tell Him about your troubles. He cares for you so much! But when you pray, you should also remember that word *empathy*—tuning in to how others feel. When you're tuned in, you'll know you aren't the only one with troubles and you aren't the only one who needs God's help. When you pray, you should pray for others. Pray for your family members, friends, and even people you don't know. If you know a specific need—someone needs healing for a sickness, comforting for sadness, help with a problem—ask God for that. If you aren't sure what someone needs, you can simply say, "God, please meet _____'s needs." God knows best what kind of help to give. Praying for someone is a wonderful way to share God's love with others. Who will you pray for today?

Dear God, please be with _____ today.
He/she needs Your help. Amen.

PRAY FOR THE WORLD

Happy is the nation whose God is the Lord. Happy
are the people He has chosen for His own.

PSALM 33:12

The world has problems. Satan is busy spreading evil around, and
we hear about it in the news. It's troubling, and maybe some of it
worries you and leaves you feeling a little helpless and afraid. Do
you know there are things you can do to make the world better?
Each time you help someone, you bring goodness into the world.
If you give someone food or gently used clothing, you are helping.
You help with your prayers. God hears when you pray about the
world's problems. He wants everyone in all nations to know and
love Him. You can pray about that. Ask God to turn all the world's
people away from evil and toward Him. It's a big prayer, but God is
already working on it. Nothing is impossible for Him.

Dear God, today I pray for all the world's people.
Lead them to You, Lord, and away from evil. Amen.

PRAY FOR OUR LEADERS

*First of all, I ask you to pray much for all men and to give thanks
for them. Pray for kings and all others who are in power over
us so we might live quiet God-like lives in peace. It is good when
you pray like this. It pleases God Who is the One Who saves.*

1 TIMOTHY 2:1–3

In a letter to his friend Timothy, Paul said to pray for those who
hold positions of power. When you pray, pray for leaders of your
country, state, and community: the president, your governor, and
your city's mayor. Pray for others in control, people like your teachers and school principal. Pray for your parents too. They have the
powerful responsibility of leading you to become an adult. Paul
said we should pray much for our leaders and give thanks for them.
You might want to add prayers for community helpers like doctors,
nurses, police officers, and firefighters.

---

*Dear God, be with those in power and help
them lead us toward You. Amen.*

AT A LOSS FOR WORDS

We do not know how to pray or what we should pray for, but the Holy Spirit prays to God for us with sounds that cannot be put into words.

ROMANS 8:26

When you face a big problem and want to tell God about it, maybe you can't find the right words. If you're at a loss for words, it's okay. God understands. Without you telling Him, God still knows what's going on and what you need. We have a helper called the Holy Spirit. The Holy Spirit is a part of God, just like Jesus is a part of God. The Holy Spirit prays to God for us when we can't find the words to say. You don't have to tell the Holy Spirit what to say because He knows. His prayer will be the best ever because the Holy Spirit is never at a loss for words. He prays perfectly all the time.

Dear Holy Spirit, I don't know how to explain what's going on. You know all about it. Please pray for me. Amen.

JESUS, TEACH US TO PRAY

*Jesus had been praying. One of His followers
said to Him, "Lord, teach us to pray."*
LUKE 11:1

Jesus taught His followers a prayer that we call the "Lord's Prayer." It is a pattern for how we should pray, so we should memorize it:

"Our Father which art in heaven, Hallowed be thy name. Thy kingdom come, Thy will be done in earth, as it is in heaven. Give us this day our daily bread. And forgive us our debts, as we forgive our debtors. And lead us not into temptation, but deliver us from evil: For thine is the kingdom, and the power, and the glory, for ever. Amen" (Matthew 6:9–13 KJV).

When you don't know what to pray, you can always pray the Lord's Prayer. Memorize it today, and keep it stored inside your heart.

Dear Jesus, Your prayer is a perfect prayer. It praises God, asks Him for what we need, requests His forgiveness, and asks Him to keep us away from sin. Thank You for teaching us to pray. Amen.

DO NOT BE AFRAID

The man who is right and good. . .will not be afraid of bad
news. His heart is strong because he trusts in the Lord.

PSALM 112:6–7

The Bible is filled with good advice. Every word is God speaking
to us. Sometimes He repeats the same advice many times because
God wants us to remember His words and put them into action. The
most repeated advice in the Bible is "Do not be afraid." Some say it's
in the Bible 365 times. Why do you think God tells us so often not
to be frightened? Because He wants us to remember that He has
power over the world. Whenever you face any kind of trouble, you
can stand up to it because God will give you strength. Being unafraid
doesn't mean you won't ever have butterflies in your stomach or
feel like running away from fear. Courage is standing strong against
what makes you afraid. It's knowing that God's Holy Spirit is inside
you wherever you are, and He will fight fear from within you.

Dear God, You have power over everything that makes me
afraid. You give me power to stand up to fear. Amen.

BUILD A FAITH LIKE DAVID'S

The Lord is my light and the One Who saves me.
Whom should I fear? The Lord is the strength
of my life. Of whom should I be afraid?

PSALM 27:1

Do you remember that little boy David who stood up to the giant soldier Goliath and knocked him down with a single stone? That boy became Israel's greatest king. David was a man with faith so strong that nothing got in his way. He said to God, "Even if an army gathers against me, my heart will not be afraid. Even if war rises against me, I will be sure of You" (Psalm 27:3). "Why should I be afraid in the days of trouble, when the sin of those who hate me is all around me?" (Psalm 49:5). "[I] will not be afraid, even if the earth is shaken and the mountains fall into the center of the sea" (Psalm 46:2). Try your best to build a faith like David's. Make your relationship with God so tight that nothing gets in its way.

Dear God, help me to have faith like David's. Amen.

FIND YOUR TRIBE

My children, you are a part of God's family.

1 JOHN 4:4

A family is more than people you're related to. God's family is made up of everyone who believes in and loves Him. One of the best ways to fight worry and fear is forming friendships with others who know and love God. They will fight for you and help with any trouble that comes your way. The Bible talks about ancient tribes who were part of God's family. A tribe is a group of people who have a common belief and leader. Its members stand up for one another. Think about forming your own tribe with other believers—friends who love God. A great place to find them is at youth groups at church. Make friends with kids you can trust to support, encourage, and pray for you. Keep adding members to your tribe. A tribe of believers can stand strong against any kind of trouble.

---

*Dear God, lead me to friends who know and love You.
Help us to encourage and support one another. Amen.*

GUARD YOUR THOUGHTS

Because they would not keep God in their thoughts anymore, He gave them up. Their minds were sinful and they wanted only to do things they should not do.

ROMANS 1:28

Satan is always sneaking around trying to get people to do things they shouldn't. He has a way of sneaking into our thoughts. That's why it's important to guard your thoughts against him. If any thought enters your mind that tells you to do something you know God wouldn't like, stop that thought! It's not coming from God. A great way to fight fear is learning to stop Satan's words as soon as you hear them. Say to him, "No. I'm not going to do that. I'm not going to listen to you." Then remember that God is more powerful than anything Satan says or does and that God is on your side. When you turn away from Satan and toward God, you can be sure everything is going to be okay.

Dear God, help me to recognize Satan's voice in my thoughts. I want to listen only to those thoughts that come from You. Amen.

FOCUS ON THE GOOD STUFF

I would have been without hope if I had not believed that I would see the loving-kindness of the Lord in the land of the living.

PSALM 27:13

You might think the world is all messed up today, but it was messed up in David's time too. He said, "I would have been without hope if I had not believed that I would see the loving-kindness of the Lord in the land of the living." David meant that if he hadn't focused on all the good stuff God was doing, he would have lost hope that anything would get better in his lifetime. When you focus on the bad stuff, you start believing things will never get any better. Don't let yourself do that. Get in the habit of looking for God's goodness. God is at work all the time doing wonderful things all over the world. Focus on that. Be a part of it too. Whenever you can, bring some goodness into the world. Give others good things to think about.

Dear God, I will focus on all the wonderful things You do. Amen.

GET ALONG WITH OTHERS

*Do that which makes you complete.... Work to get along with
others. Live in peace. The God of love and peace will be with you.*

2 CORINTHIANS 13:11

When you do your best to get along well with others, you not only
help make the world a better place, but you also help others believe
that everything will be okay. Do more than just get along with
family and friends. Be someone who encourages and supports
them. Comfort them when they feel sad. Listen to their troubles
and help when you can. Pray for them. Be positive and guide them
to see all the good things God is doing in the world. Watch your own
behavior and be a good role model. If someone gives you trouble, do
your best to bring peace into the situation. And, most of all, share
what you know about God. Help others learn to love and trust Him.

---

*Dear God, I will do my best to get along with everyone,
be a good role model, and lead them toward You. Amen.*

BE FORGIVING

"O Lord our God, You are kind and forgiving,
even when we would not obey You."

DANIEL 9:9

One of the best things about God is that He forgives us even when we don't obey Him. If we're sorry, God is quick to forgive. Maybe you have a friend who hurt your feelings or did something that made you feel angry. If your friend said, "I'm sorry," would you forgive him? Forgiveness heals hurt and angry feelings. Forgiving your friend would help both of you know that everything will be okay. If you don't feel like forgiving someone, think about Jesus. He took your sins upon Himself and died so God would forgive you. Be more like Him. Help make the world better by forgiving those who don't treat you well. Forgiveness doesn't necessarily mean you have to be friends with someone. Forgiveness is a feeling you hold inside your heart. Pray for those who hurt you. Ask God to help them.

Dear God, help me to forgive others the way You forgive me. Amen.

LOVE EACH OTHER

"I give you a new Law. You are to love each other. You must love each other as I have loved you. If you love each other, all men will know you are My followers."

JOHN 13:34–35

You've learned a lot about God. You've discovered He's greater than any problem or trouble that comes your way. You know too that God's Son, Jesus, is your best friend. He is always with you, loving you and helping you in every way. Jesus gave us a very special law to follow. He said, "You are to love each other." Love is a super powerful thing because evil can't exist where there is love. The world sees God through our love. So do your best to be kind and loving toward everyone. Love is like medicine for worries and fears. Through love, we comfort one another and remind one another that everything will be okay.

Dear Jesus, Your love comforts me, eases my worries and fears, and gives me strength. Teach me to love others the way You love me. Amen.

THE SECRET

We know that God makes all things work together for the good
of those who love Him and are chosen to be a part of His plan.
ROMANS 8:28

It's no secret there will be trouble. Jesus said so, "In the world you will have much trouble." But He added, "I have told you [this] so you may have peace in Me. Take hope! I have power over the world" (John 16:33). Sometimes you will feel a little afraid. There will be days when you worry—all humans do. But trusting God and having faith in His power will get you through every trouble. When you make Him your best friend, God will live inside your heart and be with you always. The secret to knowing everything will be okay is trusting God and believing that He will work everything out for good. Share the secret with your family and friends. Tell them, "Whatever you face today or tomorrow, God is bigger. Trust Him to help."

Dear God, I love You and trust You. With You on
my side, everything will be okay. Amen.

SCRIPTURE INDEX